To Tanya T

To God be

Dr. H.L. Morgan

BITTERNESS
A DESTROYER OF
DESTINY

Dr. H.L. Morgan

BITTERNESS
A DESTROYER OF
DESTINY

TATE PUBLISHING
AND ENTERPRISES, LLC

Bitterness: A Destroyer Of Destiny
Copyright © 2011 by Dr. H.L. Morgan. All rights reserved.

No part of this publication may be reproduced, stored in a retrieval system or transmitted in any way by any means, electronic, mechanical, photocopy, recording or otherwise without the prior permission of the author except as provided by USA copyright law.

Scripture quotations are taken from the *Holy Bible, King James Version,* Cambridge, 1769. Used by permission. All rights reserved.

The opinions expressed by the author are not necessarily those of Tate Publishing, LLC.

Published by Tate Publishing & Enterprises, LLC
127 E. Trade Center Terrace | Mustang, Oklahoma 73064 USA
1.888.361.9473 | www.tatepublishing.com

Tate Publishing is committed to excellence in the publishing industry. The company reflects the philosophy established by the founders, based on Psalm 68:11,
"The Lord gave the word and great was the company of those who published it."

Book design copyright © 2011 by Tate Publishing, LLC. All rights reserved.
Cover design by Shawn Collins
Interior design by Kenna Davis

Published in the United States of America

ISBN: 978-1-61346-048-1
1. Religion: Christian Ministry   2. Religion: General
11.11.30

ACKNOWLEDGEMENTS

All thanks goes to my Lord and Savior Jesus Christ, who gave me the strength and wisdom to complete this book. A special thanks goes to the love of my life for thirty seven years, my wife, Verlene Morgan. She really pushed me to start and complete my lifelong dream of becoming a published author. I would like to extend a thank you to my son, Dwayne Morgan, for how you share your mom and me with the people of God. Stay encouraged because you are a great father in your own right. I would like to thank everyone for their part in bringing this book together. Without your input and wisdom, this book would have never been written, with that being said, I owe you a heartfelt thank you. I would like to thank my granddaughter, Serenity Barber. Your story in this book will be appreciated by many young girls, who will read this and decide to live. Thanks to my lovely niece, Marikah. By telling your story, you are letting other young ladies know they can get through tough stuff. Sincere thanks to Lachion Morgan for your story. It shows that we must trust God through every situation. Thanks goes out to Joe Roberts. Thank you very much Nikitta for sharing your story. I know that someone will be encouraged. Sarah, I thank you for how you opened up and shared your story. Thank you so much Maria Cartwright for your story. I know it was a difficult thing for you to talk about, but you did it. Thanks to Vickie Ingram for your story. Thanks to Shauntogris Price for all your dedication and help with the drafting stages of this book. Special thanks to Dr. Lee Moore, Dr. Louise Moore, and Maranath College of Theology, God used my connection to the two of you and enrollment into college as a vessel to help me accomplish the goal of becoming a published writer. Thank you to Bishop Donval Miller for being unselfish and connecting me to the right people that helped me become a published author. My deepest thanks and gratitude goes to the Tabernacle of Joy church family for all your support.

TABLE OF CONTENTS

Introduction 9
How Does Bitterness Enter In? 13
Guarding the Gates to Bitterness............ 19
Guarding Your Spirit Against Offences 54
Getting to the Root 62
The Effects of Bitterness................... 70
How Bitterness Affects Your Health 73
How Bitterness Affects Your Spirit 80
The Healing Power of Forgiveness 84
My Story 94
Personal Experiences of Others 100
Twelve Suggestions to Conquer Bitterness.... 155
Scriptures on Bitterness 163
Work Cited............................... 169

INTRODUCTION

This book is based on my own experience with this binding and controlling spirit of bitterness. My prayer is that everyone who reads this book will get a clear understanding of how detrimental and dangerous this demonic spirit really is to a child of God. For many years, this spirit controlled and ruined the early stages of my life. There are so many Christians who are dealing with or have dealt with bitterness. This spirit is destroying families, churches, homes, businesses, and the personal lives of many people. We, as the saints of God, must get a handle on this spirit. Allowing this spirit to have dominion over our lives keeps us from enjoying the life that Jesus Christ died for us to have. The Apostle Paul instructs us in the epistle to the church of Ephesus how to combat this spirit: "Let all bitterness and wrath, and clamour, and evil speaking be put away from you with all malice; And be kind one to another, tenderhearted, forgiving one even as God for the sake of Christ hath forgiven you" (Ephesians 4:31–32). I don't profess to be a hunter; but anyone who participates in the sport of hunting or trapping animals know that in order to catch an animal, you must bait the trap with something that the prey loves and you must also camouflage the trap so he does not see it. Satan is the same way. He is a master of disguises. "And no marvel Satan himself is transformed into an angel of light" (2 Corinthians 11:14). This scripture sheds light on the enemy we are fighting. Bitterness is a spirit that slowly takes over your life, mind, and soul. It will begin to dictate your actions. Bitterness will begin to influence how you respond to people and situations that arise in everyday life.

You might ask how I know this much about this evil spirit. Well, for many years, the spirit of bitterness was a major stronghold in my life. I did not have to look it up in a dictionary or go to Wikipedia to find the definition because I have lived it.

The Bible says offence must come. Given this piece of knowledge, it is impossible to believe that we will live in this world without becoming offended. The important thing to do when an offence comes is to guard your heart, mind, and spirit. The failure to release the hurt, pain, and anger the offence might have brought to your heart, mind, and spirit will cause you to become ineffective and uncaring in your Christian walk.

Out of the heart the mouth speaks. Dealing with offence is definitely a matter of the heart. In order for someone to have the ability to offend you, there must be a level of respect, love, and trust for him/her. Being offended is not a pleasurable emotion to experience. Many of us allow those feelings of hurt to develop into bitterness and resentment. It is important that we do not allow those hurts to define our character and affect our ability to love. Bitterness harbored in our hearts will cause us to disconnect from the people we love, organizations we have devoted our life's work to, and from anything that has the potential to cause us pain again. God is love; and to be an effective vessel for his use, we must show love to all people.

Instead of allowing the spirit of offence to take root in our heart and create grudges, we should overlook the issue that caused the offence and forgive. Forgiving a person does not mean that you forget what a person has done. Forgiveness means you no longer allow what has happened to affect your actions, attitude, and frame of mind. The inability to forgive stops God's plan for our lives. God says, "If we do not forgive, we will not be forgiven." The ability to forgive allows God's grace to rest, rule, and abide in our lives. We need to realize there are going to be times when we are going to offend someone, intentionally or unintentionally, because we are imperfect people. Since we are also guilty of being an offender, we must quickly forgive and repent so that nothing enters our hearts. The golden rule is to treat others the way we want to be treated. So it is vital that we set an example of God's grace, love, kindness, and forgiveness when it comes to dealing with people who have offended us. Don't accept those things in your hearts, in your relationships, or in your house. Kick them out.

HOW DOES BITTERNESS ENTER IN?

The spirit of bitterness has a mission from hell, and that is to make Christians' lives as miserable and sorrowful as it can. My questions to you as a Christian are, Have you ever been rejected by others? Have you ever been wronged by anyone? Have you ever had a loved one die and you turned your grief toward God?" "Beloved avenge not yourselves, but rather give place to wrath, for it is written 'vengeance I will repay' saith the Lord" (Romans 12:19). In order to fully understand what bitterness is, let's explore the meaning of the word in the Greek. The first word needing to be defined is *pikros*. *Pikros* is defined as "bitter, sharp, or pointed." The second word needing to be defined is *pikria*. *Pikria* is defined as "bitterness or poison." So from these two words, bitterness would mean to be resentful, to be in a poisonous frame of mind, to be in a hostile, or a combative position. There will be many times in our lives that we will be offended, hurt by loved ones, friends, associates, and even church members. Jesus address this issue in the gospel of Luke 17:1: "Then said he unto the disciples, *'It is impossible'* but that offences will come; but woe unto him through whom they come. *He* said to his disciples, 'Hard trials and temptations are bound to come, but to bad for whosoever brings them on'" (Message Bible). Solomon, in the book of Proverbs, tells of an offended brother and how hard it is to reach such a person. "A brother offended is harder to be won than a strong city; and their contentions are like the bars of a castle" (Proverbs 18:19). The undertaking of dealing with an offended person is a great task to accomplish, and it takes the wisdom of God to accomplish this mission.

We have very good examples of people who allowed bitterness to destroy and ruin their destiny. Let's first look at the example of the life of Cain. It is common biblical knowledge that Cain got bitter and envious of his brother, Abel's offering to God. The need for this bitterness was not necessary because God gave him an opportunity to make it right. God told him, "If thou doest well shalt not thou be accepted." God was giving him a chance to correct the mistake he made in his offering choice. Instead of repenting and correcting his fault, he killed his brother. Bitterness will keep us from being our brother's keeper.

A second example where bitterness got the best of family members is the story of Jacob. We also have the twin brother of Jacob, whose name is Esau. His bitterness came from his own carelessness of protecting the birthright of the firstborn. He sold it to his younger brother, Jacob, for a pot of venison soup. Joseph's brothers' bitterness derived from the favor shown to Joseph by Jacob their father.

> Now Israel loved Joseph more than all his children, because he was the son of his old age; and he made him a coat of many colors. And when his brethren saw that their father loved him more than all his brethren, they hated him and could not speak peaceably unto him.
> Genesis 37:3–4

This did not end the bitterness and the hatred that Joseph's brothers had toward him. This lets us know that if this spirit is not dealt with, it only gets deeper and much more difficult to handle.

> And Joseph dreamed a dream, and he told it his brethren: and they hated him yet the more. And his brethren said to him "Shalt thou indeed reign over us? or shall thou indeed have dominion over us?" And they hated him yet the more for his dreams, and for his words. And his brethren envied him, but his father observed the saying.
>
> Genesis 37:5, 8, 11

This is another example how detrimental this spirit is to a family. In this story, their bitterness turned into hatred. Absalom's bitterness against his father, David, derived from a situation he did not handle properly. Naomi, in her return, came into the city of Bethlehem a bitter woman after losing her husband and two sons in a famine in Moab. Hannah, the mother of Samuel, got bitter because she could have no children. King Saul was bitter about the relationship that Jonathan, his son, and David had. Job's wife became bitter when she saw her children dead and a healthy husband sick. She saw no hope; and when we see no hope in our situation, it breeds bitterness and resentment. Many more of these characters we will discuss in later chapters of the book. When I began to really study the lives of the people that I just mentioned and the ones we will discuss later, we will see how they allowed this spirit to destroy their life and their destiny. That is why I know that this is a serious issue in the body of Christ. I would go as far to say that 85 to 90 percent of many church conflicts, many divorces, and family arguments come from the spirit of bitterness. We must always remember that this spirit works like the undercurrent in a river; you only know when you come to an undercurrent, when you feel something in the water that is not seen pulling you under. This is the way bitterness is. It pulls you under because it hides and mask itself with so many disguises. It is God's will that we live in peace with him and others.

"Follow peace with all men and holiness, without which no man shall see the Lord" (Hebrews 12:14).

"If it be possible, as much as lieth in you, live peaceably with all men" (Romans 12:18).

"Peace I leave with you, my peace I give unto you: not as the world giveth, give I unto you. Let not your heart be troubled, neither let it be afraid" (John 16:27).

These three verses let us know how serious and how important it is for us to get control of this spirit in our lives.

GUARDING THE GATES TO BITTERNESS

We will discover in this chapter the gates that allow bitterness to enter into our lives. There are four gates we want to research: the gate of resentment, the gate of unforgiveness, the gate of the mouth, and the gate of pride. We must allow God to close these gates in our lives that cause us so much agony and pain. These things keep us bound to our past and never let us move on. One day, I got tired of this cycle and decided to do something about it.

Bitterness is a common issue that any adult or even child may deal with at some point in life. Bitterness is commonly associated with unforgiveness. What is unforgiveness? In order to understand what unforgiveness is, you must be able to identify what it is not. The definition of *forgive* is "to give up or cease to feel resentment; to grant relief from payment or pardon, which means to excuse an offense without executing penalty." When you forgive someone, you are willing to let go of the offense, any and all resentment, and show mercy. When you choose not to forgive, you are doing the exact opposite. Unforgiveness can have some harmful effects on your life if you continue to harbor those feelings of resentment. When you store unforgiveness or resentment in your heart, it is like a seed that grows whether you are aware of it or not.

At first, it will start out with anger. It will then turn into resentment. The final product will be bitterness. Bitterness will begin to affect your mind, thoughts, and how you see others. As it begins to grow, it hardens your heart and then spreads to other areas in your life. After a long period of time, you will become a different person. Instead of enjoying the blessings in your life, you will become full of anger and cynicism toward life and people. You will become a hard person to love and it will become harder for you to show love. How can we forgive when we don't want to? We must learn to see ourselves and our situations in the light of God's word. Bitterness often promotes a sense of prolonging a negative situation. We have emotions that help us relate to what is happening to us. We must determine what the root cause of our bitterness is in order to achieve forgiveness. Hebrews 12:15 (NIV) states, "See to it that no one misses the grace of God and that no bitter root grows up to cause trouble and defile many." Bitterness starts from the inside and slowly works to the outside. It will begin in your heart and then manifest itself in our attitudes and actions. A bitter person hurts not only other people, but they first and foremost cannot enjoy the grace of God. This is because God's grace is dependent on our forgiveness and grace toward others. The resentful, bitter person focuses on getting what they deserve. Unresolved anger can be a root of bitterness. Anger is a natural emotion when we perceive that we have been treated unfairly or our rights have been violated. Anger should be handled in a healthy way, although most times we deal with it by shouting, cussing, or grumbling.

Bitterness usually takes root when we don't deal with anger. When anger is not dealt with it stays an issue. Many relationships don't end because there is one big issue that arose, but because individuals simply got tired of the small, unresolved issues. When our expectations are not met, we tend to become bitter. We begin to experience disillusionment when relationships did not live up to our expectations. We begin to present the attitude of blame. Our bodies are designed with the capacity to heal naturally once we get hurt. However, this is not always the case emotionally. Hurts that are undeserved or deep and caused by a trusted person are the types of hurts that can't just be shaken off. These hurts don't just go away. Healing takes time with a lot of mental and emotional discipline. No matter how valid our feelings are from the start, whether they be anger or hurt, we begin to hurt ourselves and the people around us. The positive steps of being free from bitterness begin with acceptance. If the root cause of your bitterness is unresolved anger that has piled up without being addressed, learn to express your disappointment. We must learn how to communicate and resolve issues.

Forgiveness is God's answer to life's unfairness. The only way we can unload all of the hurts we have experienced is to focus on God's grace and forgiveness of our sins. Learning to forgive deep hurts is a slow process, happening one day at a time. There are four main reasons why we have to forgive. Freedom; through forgiveness, sets you free from hurt and pain of the past. You are no longer in bondage to it but you can move forward in your future. Restoration happens by forgiving. You are able to be restored back to where you were before the incident took place but with more strength and wisdom from the experience.

You're no longer hindered by the past but can walk freely in God being restored and redeemed. The healing process does not come quickly. You slowly begin to feel joy again. You are no longer bound by your suffering. You are delivered and healed. The Bible says that if we do not forgive, God will not forgive us (Matthew 6:14–15).

Forgiveness brings peace within your heart, and you are at peace with God. Evaluate your life situation. Ask yourself honestly if you are struggling with unforgiveness or bitterness. How has it affected your life, your heart, your attitude, your point of view, and the way you treat yourself and others? If you find that you indeed are suffering from bitterness, I encourage you to seek forgiveness and ask God to help you. First, you must confess it to God. By confessing it to Him, you are acknowledging that you were hurt by the situation or person but you realize that you need to forgive in spite of how you feel in order to be restored. Allow God to comfort you so that your relationship with Him can be re-established. If you have been estranged from God, repent and return unto Him. We need Jesus to be restored and to forgive. Apart from God, we can do nothing. Then you must forgive and let it go. The Bible says, "Cast all your cares upon Him for He cares for you." Letting go is now a matter of faith. When your heart has moved beyond the hurt and is in the place of restoration, you will remember but will no longer be in bondage to it. It will take time to get to this point; but if you truly forgive and let go, you will have great relief from the pain and hope to keep moving forward in your life with joy. You will also need to have fellowship with positive people who will impact this healing and process of forgiveness in a positive manner. Continue to talk about what you have been through, and allow God to comfort you through this phase.

The Gate of Resentment

What does it mean to be resentful? A resentful person has a sense of injury, constant anger arising from being wronged, or the continual showing of ill will or injured emotions. "And when his brethren saw that that their father loved Joseph more than all his brethren, they hated him and could not speak peaceably unto him" (Genesis 37:4). When we study this scripture, it shows us how resentment can go deeply into the soul. It was so deep that they could not speak peaceably to Joseph; in other words, they could not have a decent conversation with him. The first sign of trouble comes from a coat of many colors that their father gave him: so their animosity comes from his father showing favoritism by only giving Joseph a coat. It is amazing what we can have resentment over. "And Joseph dreamed a dream, and he told it to his brethren, and they hated him yet the more" (Genesis 37:5). The dream that God showed him is that he shall rule over them at some point in life. God holds the future, not men. All his brothers could see was this little, seventeen–year–old kid saying he is going to rule over them. This lets us know that God has a destiny for us, and the scripture shows us how deep this hatred or resentment goes. They hated him yet the more for his dreams and his words. "And he dreamed yet another dream, and told it to his brethren, and said, Behold I have dreamed a dream more; and behold, the sun and the moon and the eleven stars made obeisance to me" (Genesis 37:9). In this dream, God extended Joseph's dream that he would be ruling over the whole family. The reaction of the brothers this time was to envy him, but the father's reaction was that he observed the saying. "And his brethren envied him, but the father observed the saying" (Genesis 37:11). The hatred and resentment is now getting deeper. Envy is the next step to murder.

> And when they saw him afar off, even before he came near unto them, they conspired against him to slay him. And they said one to another, "Behold this dreamer comes. Come now therefore, and let us slay him, and cast him into some pit and we will say some evil beast hath devoured him: and we shall see what will become of his dreams."
>
> Genesis 37:18–20

This verse also lets us know that man cannot destroy the plans that God has placed over your life. As we will see later, every dream that Joseph dreamed came to pass.

The Gate of Unforgiveness

This is another gate that we, as Christians, must close shut in our lives. What is unforgiveness? What does it mean to be unforgiving? The act of unforgiving is refusing to release a grudge or an aught against someone. Jesus, in the gospel of Matthew, gives us a story of forgiveness and unforgiveness.

> Therefore is the kingdom of heaven likened unto a certain king, which would take account of his servants. And when he had begun to reckon, one

> was brought unto him, which owed him ten thousand talents [10,000]. Forasmuch as he had not to pay, his lord commanded him to be sold, and his wife, and children, and all that he had and payment to be made. The servant therefore fell down and worshipped him, saying, Lord, have patience with me, and I will pay thee all. Then the lord of the servant was moved with compassion, and loosed him and forgave him of the debt.
>
> Matthew 18:23–27

There are a couple of things that I noticed about this parable. The amount of the debt of sin, which says to me that all of us have a sin debt, we could not pay. My life or your life was not sufficient to pay for our sins. Jesus never tells us what the infraction was. I believe he's letting all of us know that we all have a sin debt. Knowing them is not as important as repenting for them. The lord of this servant knew that he would never be able to repay such a huge amount, so he had compassion and forgave the debt. It also appears to me that Jesus was saying carrying unforgiveness is like being in debt. It is a weight and a burden. We must learn to forgive quickly. This same servant had a fellow servant that owed him way less than he owed his lord, but let us look at the reaction that he showed his friend.

But the same servant went out, and found one of his fellow servants, which owed him a hundred pence and laid hands on him and took him by the throat, saying "Pay me that thou owest." And his fellow servant fell down at his feet, and besought him saying, "Have patience with me, and I will pay thee all." And he would not: but went and cast him into prison, till he should pay the debt. So when his fellow servants saw what was done, they were very sorry, and told unto their lord all that was done. Then his lord, after that he had called him, said unto him, "Oh thou wicked servant, I forgave thee all that debt, because thou desiredst me. Shouldest not thou also have had compassion on thy fellow servant, even as I had pity on thee?" And his lord was wroth, and delivered him to the tormentors, till he should pay all that was due unto him. So likewise shall my heavenly Father do also unto you, if you from your hearts forgive not everyone his brother their trespasses.

Matthew 18: 28–35

When I read these verses, it hit home how important it is for us to forgive one another with all the sins we have committed. I'm also reminded of the times that I have been out of the will of God and how He had compassion on me and forgave me. From the parable we read, it is obvious that if I don't forgive from the heart, I will be tormented and not forgiven by God for my sins. We must show others the same grace that was shown unto us.

The Gate of the Mouth

Generally, when people get their own way with others, they do it with words. They virtually compel others to agree with their point of view, give them what they want, do what they ask, and buy what they are selling. The seduction/assault of words is continuous. There is enormous power in the meaning of the words, and thier impact on the people hearing them. The words elicit emotional responses that manipulate other people's thinking and behavior.

These manipulations have been defined as fallacious arguments. While the arguments appear to relate to the subject, they do not. In most cases, they have little to do with the subject at all. There are thirty or so of these misleading and deceptive arguments.

The danger lies in the fact that decisions based on them are not based on truth, common sense, logic, legality, one's best interests, or right and wrong but on emotions, favoring those who put forth the more powerful arguments. They are designed to benefit someone else. In the book of Judges, you will find a story where the words of one woman seduced a man of God to nothing. The words that flow from our lips can create or destroy. That is why we must constantly be mindful of what we say.

> And it came to pass, when she pressed him daily with her words, and urged him, so that his soul was vexed unto death. That he told her all his heart, and said unto her, that hath not came a razor on my head; for I have been a Nazarite unto God from my mother's womb; if I be shaven, then my strength will be gone from me, and I shall become week as other men.
>
> Judges 16:16–17

Delilah urged him and she pressed him with her words daily, which means she kept telling and asking Samson the same question every day. Now turn that same principal around to say good things every day. Imagine what type of impact we would have on the world, on our children, on our nation, and on our families. Samson told Delilah three lies before he told the truth because words play on our emotions.

As emotions are constantly changing, opinions and decisions based on them also change. They are not stable, dependable, or consistent over time. At any moment, they can be overthrown by someone else's more compelling argument. Unknowingly making choices based on emotional appeals and logical tricks, one allows others to control their thinking and their behavior, setting themselves up to be used for someone else's interests.

Another gate that must be guarded or even closed is the mouth. This particular gate has caused many of us to lose relationships, blessings, and families; and it will even destroy our destiny if we don't gain control of it. "Death and life are in the power of the tongue: and they that love it shall eat the fruit thereof" (Proverbs 18:21). The Message Bible gives us this paraphrase of this scripture: "Words kill, Words give life they're either poison or fruit you choose." For the past year or more, I have been watching what I say and how I say it. It has been amazing to me how negative I talked sometimes. Now that I realize how powerful words are and the creative nature of the words we speak, we must be diligent to correct our speech. The Apostle James gives us insight on how dangerous an untamed tongue can be to a child of God: "And the tongue is a fire, a world of iniquity: so is the tongue among our members, that it defileth the whole body, and setteth on fire the course of nature; and it is set on fire of hell" (James 3:6). The analogy that James uses is very fitting to the nature of an untamed tongue. It is like a fire that has no boundaries or is uncontrolled. Fire is a great thing if used in the right place and under the right circumstances. This same fire that is a good thing, when out of control, can burn houses down, burn people up, or set a whole forest on fire. The tongue is a valuable member to the body; but out of control, it can bring destruction to a family, church, marriage, and the life of a child. "Only by pride cometh contention, but with the well advised is wisdom" (Proverbs 13:10). In the great book of Ruth, this woman of God had to deal with some grief. We will see how she handled the grief process. Yes, I said process because that is what God uses to get us through any type of grief situation, whether it is the death of a child, death of a spouse, divorce, or being rejected by people and family.

> Turn again, my daughters, go your way; for I am too old to have a husband. If I should have a husband also tonight, and should also bear sons would you tarry for them till they are grown? Would you stay for them from having a husband? Nay, my daughters, for it grieveth me

much for your sakes that the hand of the Lord is gone against me.

Ruth 1:12–13

From reading these passages of Scripture, we already see into the bitterness that Naomi carried, the death of her husband and the death of her two sons, Mahon and Chilion. There are a few things that Naomi allows to come out of her mouth that let us know the depth of her bitterness. She blames God for the things that have happened to her. She says the hand of the Lord is against her. She says, "Don't call me Naomi. It means pleasant." She does not feel her life is pleasant anymore. She said, "Call me Mara, which means bitter because the Lord has dealt bitterly with me." If Naomi would have known what the Lord had in store for her, I believe she would have talked differently. Before you pass judgment on Naomi, all of us have felt like she did. Whenever you feel like murmuring and griping about things, watch out. Such an unthankful, doubtful, negative attitude might not only be an indication of bitterness, but of backsliding as well. Even if you haven't actually turned your back on the Lord, you're turning back in your heart when you start yielding to that feeling of doubt, murmuring and being critical of everybody else. When people start picking out others' faults, covering their own, murmuring and griping about everything, and complaining instead of praising the Lord for what they have, it's a dangerous sin.

Even if you don't end up completely backsliding, you'll certainly lose your inspiration and the Lord's anointing, if you go around voicing complaints and resentments like that. You can't keep complaining, criticizing, murmuring, and bellyaching about things and still keep God's Holy Spirit in you. You just can't do it. You'll wind up like Saul. The Spirit left him, and he became so hardened of heart and cold that he didn't even know it was gone. He didn't realize he had lost it. When someone's going around murmuring and constantly being critical of everything, it shows that they've been entertaining the devil's lies in their mind and heart. "For out of the abundance of the heart the mouth speaketh" (Matthew 12:34). They then become a witness for the devil. If your heart is filled with negative thoughts, sooner or later, you'll mouth them; and that's when you really begin to pull others down too. One reason people complain and and bellyache and criticize is because they know that they're not making it themselves and that they haven't got the victory. They know that they're failing because of their own unyieldedness or rebelliousness. Rather than really trying to make it stop failing and do better, they start looking around for something to justify, excuse, or vindicate themselves. So they frequently accuse and blame everybody else for their own faults and failures and will freely criticize everybody else but themselves. Such murmuring is virtually the voice of the enemy and his doubts; and a critical spirit like that sows dissension, disunity, and discord amongst brethren, one of the seven abominations to God (Proverbs 6:16–19). So God certainly won't and can't bless people who allow themselves to fall into such a sorry state. In fact, if you sin by murmuring against God and complaining about your life, circumstances, living conditions, your shepherds, or your brethren, God might just let you stay there much longer than He'd originally planned. A good example of this is how He dealt with the children of Israel when they murmured against Him—until you learn to be thankful and patient "Tribulation worketh patience" (Romans 5:3). No matter how great your trial might be, if you just have faith to trust God to bring you out of that difficulty, you won't murmur and complain. You'll rejoice , praise –and thank Him even for the trial, because you know He is able to save and deliver you. Praise the Lord!

If there is any universal failure among mankind, it is the misuse of the tongue. It is little wonder that one of the most frequently discussed subjects in the book of Proverbs is the use of the tongue. If our problem with the tongue is a common one, it is also an especially crucial one. For one thing, the tongue is capable of achieving either great good or great evil. Furthermore, the words we speak cannot be taken back once spoken. It is impossible to undo damage done by the tongue.

The beginning of strife is like letting out water, so abandon the quarrel before it breaks out (Proverbs 17:14). A brother offended is harder to be won than a strong city, and contentions are like the bars of a castle (Proverbs 18:19). Finally, James suggests in his epistle that the key to the control of our entire body is to be found in the control of the mouth.

We all stumble in many ways. If any one does not stumble in what he says, he is a perfect man, able to bridle the whole body as well. Now if we put the bits into the horses' mouths so that they may obey us, we direct their entire body as well (James 3:2–3). Failure to guard the gate of your mouth can lead to a lot of dangerous and deadly situations in the spirit and life. The book of Proverbs lets us know how failure to guard the gate of our mouth can destroy our family and ourselves. An unguarded gate will cause a person to breach the confidence amongst friends, families, and co-workers. He who goes about as a talebearer reveals secrets, but he who is trustworthy conceals a matter (Proverbs 11:13). Argue your case with your neighbor; and do not reveal the secret of another, lest he who hears it reproach you and the evil report about you not pass away (Proverbs 25:9–10). Secondly, commitments will be made in haste.

> My son, if you have become surety for your neighbor, Have given a pledge for a stranger, If you have been snared with the words of your mouth, Have been caught with the words of your mouth, Do this then, my son, and deliver yourself; Since you have come into the hand of your neighbor, Go, humble yourself, and importune your neighbor. Do not give sleep to your eyes, Nor slumber to your eyelids; Deliver yourself like a gazelle from the hunter's hand, And like a bird from the hand of the fowler.
> Proverbs 6:1–5

It is a snare for a man to say rashly, "It is holy," and after the vows make inquiry (Proverbs 20:25). Contention and strife are continually around when Christians fail to guard their mouths and tongues. Keeping away from strife is an honor for a man, but any fool will quarrel (Proverb 20:3). Attempting to correct or instruct a fool is pointless when they have failed to guard their mouth. Do not speak in the hearing of a fool, for he will despise the wisdom of your words (Proverbs 23:9).When a wise man has a controversy with a foolish man, the foolish man either rages or laughs; and there is no rest (Proverbs 29:9). Many youth are unaware of the need to watch the words that are coming out their mouths, and this act causes them to miss out on the blessing of God due to the words coming out their mouths. He who curses his father or his mother, his lamp will go out in time of darkness (Proverbs 20:20 and 30:11). An unguarded mouth is subject to not being completely honest. A false witness will not go unpunished, and he who tells lies will not escape (Proverbs19:5). A rascally witness makes a mockery of justice, and the mouth of the wicked spreads iniquity (Proverbs 19:28). A lying tongue hates those it crushes, and a flattering mouth works ruin (Proverbs 26:28).He who rebukes a man will afterward find more favor than he who flatters with the tongue (Proverbs 28:23). A man who flatters his neighbor is spreading a net for his steps (Proverbs 29:5). The words of a whisperer are like dainty morsels, and they go down into the innermost parts of the body (Proverbs 18:8). He who goes about as a slanderer reveals secrets, therefore do not associate with a gossip (Proverbs 20:19).

The north wind brings forth rain, and the backbiting tongue an angry countenance (Proverbs 25:23). Put away from you a deceitful mouth, and put devious lips far from you (Proverbs 4:24). A worthless person, a wicked man, is the one who walks with a false mouth, who winks with his eyes, who signals with his feet, who points with his fingers (Proverbs 6:12–13). Lastly, an unguarded mouth will cause you to boast on yourself. Like clouds and wind without rain is a man who boasts of his gifts falsely (Proverbs 25:14).

Let others praise you and not your own mouth, a stranger and not your own lips (Proverbs 27:2).

The Gate of Pride

The spirit of pride is a great contributor to bitterness because pride will only let us look to the wellness of ourselves. It is a spirit of selfishness. Pride keeps us from admitting we are bitter about something. We must confess this to God so our destiny will not be hindered. "In the mouth of the foolish is a rod of pride: but the lips of the wise shall preserve them" (Proverbs 14:3). "Whoso privily slandereth his neighbor, him will I cut off: him that hath a high look and a proud heart will I not suffer" (Psalms 101:5). When we act proud and foolish, God is against us. He knows our heart. Jesus gives us a parable in the book of Luke that shows us how dangerous pride is to our walk with the Lord.

> Two men went up into temple to pray; the one a Pharisee, and the other a publican. The Pharisee stood and prayed thus with himself, God, I thank thee that I am not as other men are extortioners, unjust, adulterers, or even as this publican. I fast twice in the week I give tithes of all I possess. And the publican, standing afar off, would not lift up so much as his eyes unto heaven, but smote upon his breast, saying God be merciful to me a sinner. I tell you, this man went down to his house justified rather than the other: For everyone that exalteth himself shall be abased; and he that humbleth himself shall be exalted.
>
> Luke 18:10–14

In this parable, Jesus shows us how pride can destroy our prayer life. It will not allow us to pray to God with a honest heart. This spirit makes us critical and very judgmental. As this parable tells us, this man began to look down on the publican and tried to justify himself to God. This demonstration of pride is the pride that all of us have. It makes us justify ourselves. "Pride goeth before destruction, and a haughty spirit before a fall," the Bible says (Proverbs 16:18). It is true. When a heart of pride lifts itself up, a vision for successful life is destroyed. The pride of a haughty spirit always sets a person up for a great tumble into "the sin which doth so easily beset us" (Hebrews 12:1). From there, it is downward and downward; and unless checked through genuine repentance, it carries such a self–deluded, arrogant, deceived sinner all the way into the pit of the lowest hell. "Before destruction the heart of man is haughty, and before honour is humility" (Proverbs 18:12).Toward such prideful ones, the God of heaven declares, "For a fire is kindled in mine anger, and shall burn unto the lowest hell, and shall consume the earth with her increase, and set on fire the foundations of the mountains" (Deuteronomy 32:22). It is out of such a place that pollution of the heart, called pride leads us to hell, that the psalmists prayed, "For great is thy mercy toward me: and thou hast delivered my soul from the lowest hell" (Psalm 86:13).Yes, "pride goeth before destruction" all right and brings with it a further fall." The wicked, through the pride of his countenance, will not seek after God: God is not in all his thoughts" (Psalm 10:4). Such is the state of the inner soul of the pride of man. Such is the sin of pride that always goes before even that most loathsome of sins called sodomy. "For thy sister Sodom was not mentioned by thy mouth in the day of thy pride" (Ezekiel 16:56). And to such sinners infected with what the Bible calls the pride of life, God scolds:

> And I will break the pride of your power; and I will make your heaven as iron, and your earth as brass. And your strength shall be spent in vain: for your land shall not yield her increase, neither shall the trees of the land yield their fruits. And if ye walk contrary unto me, and will not hearken unto me; I will bring seven times more plagues upon you according to your sins. I will also send wild beasts among you, which shall rob you of your children, and destroy your cattle, and make you few in number; and your high ways shall be desolate.
>
> Leviticus 26:19–22

There is a story in the Bible about a great king who suffered from pride. His name was Nebuchadnezzar."The king spake, and said, 'Is not this great Babylon, that I have built for the house of the kingdom by the might of my power, and for the honour of my majesty?'" (Daniel 4:30). Note the utter selfish pride in such a claim. Fact of the matter is, "God is the judge: he putteth down one, and setteth up another" (Psalm 75:7) and "the most High ruleth in the kingdom of men, and giveth it to whomsoever he will, and setteth up over it the basest of men" (Daniel 4:17). Yet King Nebuchadnezzar knew not the God of heaven and had no knowledge of His sovereign will working in the earth.

> While the word was in the king's mouth, there fell a voice from heaven, saying, "O king Nebuchadnezzar, to thee it is spoken; The kingdom is departed from thee." The same hour was the thing fulfilled upon Nebuchadnezzar: and he was driven from men, and did eat grass as oxen, and his body was wet with the dew of heaven, till his hairs were grown like eagles' feathers, and his nails like birds' claws. And at the end of the days I Nebuchadnezzar lifted up mine eyes unto heaven, and mine understanding returned unto me, and I blessed the most High, and I praised and honoured him that liveth for ever, whose dominion is an everlasting dominion, and his kingdom is from generation to generation. And all the inhabitants of the earth are reputed as nothing: and he doeth according to his will in the army of heaven, and among the inhabitants

> of the earth: and none can stay his hand, or say unto him, "What doest thou?" At the same time my reason returned unto me; and for the glory of my kingdom, mine honour and brightness returned unto me; and my counselors and my lords sought unto me; and I was established in my kingdom, and excellent majesty was added unto me. Now I Nebuchadnezzar praise and extol and honour the King of heaven, all whose works are truth, and his ways judgment: and those that walk in pride he is able to abase.
>
> Daniel 4:31, 33–37

There is another king in the Bible who suffered from the spirit of pride named Uzziah. He became king at sixteen years old and served as Judah's king for fifty-two years. But one day, his pride got in his way. He did a service he was not called to do. He offered incense in the temple, which was only to be done by the priest. When they tried to correct him, the Bible says he got angry and for his disobedience, leprosy began to attack his body. And the Bible says he was a leper until his death.

> But when he was strong, his heart was lifted up to his destruction; for he transgressed against the Lord his God, and went into the temple of the

Lord to burn incense upon the altar of incense. And Azariah the priest went in after him, fourscore priests of the Lord, that were valiant men: And they withstood Uzziah the king, and said unto him, "It appertained not thee, Uzziah, to burn incense unto the Lord, but to the priests the sons of Aaron, that are consecrated to burn incense: go out of the sanctuary for thou hath trespassed, neither shall it be for thine honor from the Lord God." Then was Uzziah wroth, and had a censer in his hand to burn the incense, and while he was wroth with the priests, the leprosy even rose in his forehead before the priests in the house of the Lord, from beside the incense altar. And Azariah the chief priest, and all the priests, looked upon him and behold he was leprous in his forehead, and they thrust him out from thence; yea he himself hasted also to go out, because the Lord had smitten him. And Uzziah the king was a leper unto the day of his death, and he dwelt in a several house, being a leper; for he was cut off from the house of the Lord.

2 Chronicles 26:16–21

This great king's pride destroyed everything he had done.

The Gate of your Mind

The easiest way to prevent something from growing in your garden is to not let it get sown or planted there in the first place. The best way to prevent any roots of bitterness from springing up in your life is to not let any bitter, critical, or negative seeds find their way into the garden of your mind and heart. This means you have got to guard your thoughts and resist the devil when he tries to sow his evil seeds and thoughts in your mind.

We all go through experiences sometimes where we listen to the enemy instead of the Lord. In fact, the Lord lets us hear the devil's voice and thoughts sometimes, even if it's only a test to see if we will receive or reject it. Not all voices are of God, and you must learn to "try the spirits" (1 John 4:1). Beloved believe not every spirit, but try the spirits whether they are of God: because many false prophets are gone out into the world, so make sure that what you're hearing is of the Lord. If it's not according to His Word or causes you to be discontent or bitter, dissatisfied or unhappy, or critical of yourself or others, these things are not of the Lord. You must rebuke the enemy in Jesus' name when he tempts you with these kinds of negative thoughts. You can't keep the devil from saying things to you and tempting you to harbor negative thoughts or thoughts against others or even against the Lord.

He will always try to speak to you and try to get you to let him have his evil way. Even if you're unable to keep from hearing him speak sometimes, you can always keep from doing what he says. A lot of people feel bad and think that they must be terribly wicked because they think an unloving or sinful thought. But as my mother used to say, "Even though you can't keep the birds from flying over your head, you can keep them from making a nest in your hair." You can't keep the devil from tempting you and casting his fiery darts at you and talking to you; however, you don't have to talk back to him or open the door and invite him and all his little devils and doubts in. You can mentally fight against evil thinking and negative thoughts. Resist all such thoughts and think positively. Think out loud by either quoting scriptures or singing hymns or good gospel songs. You can't very well quote Scripture and talk positively or sing out loud and have those other negative thoughts going through your head at the same time. When a room is dark, you don't go around trying to chase the darkness out of the room. You just let the light in, and the light chases out the darkness. So the way to get rid of temptations and negative thoughts is to think of good Godly things. Read your Bible, pray, and think about Jesus. Then you don't even have time to think the other thoughts, which is why Isaiah says, "Thou wilt keep him in perfect peace whose mind is stayed on Thee, because he trusteth in Thee" (Isaiah 26:3). If you keep your mind on Jesus, you don't have time to think about these other things. Fill your mind with the wonderful, powerful Word of God and you won't have room for that darkness. Fill your mind with the light of God's Word, and the darkness will flee. Don't even listen to the devil's lies because if you do, the same thing that happened to Eve will happen to you. Don't listen to his doubts and his fears and his discouragement and his temptations and all the rest. Sock him with the Word of God. When you're tempted to think negative, resentful, critical, or hateful thoughts against your brothers or sisters, remember that the devil is the accuser of the saints and he will always try to accuse others and exaggerate their faults to you. He will even take innocent, unintentional remarks or acts and twist them and make them sound a lot worse than they really are. But once you can recognize that such negative and critical thoughts are the enemy's attacks against you to separate and divide you from your brothers and sisters in the Lord, and then you can slam the door on all such thoughts and take a definite positive stand against them. When you have faith in God and His Word, then you know that the devil is a liar; and when those kinds of bad and bitter thoughts come into your mind, you know it's the devil speaking. So just say, "I resist you, Satan, in Jesus' name. I resist you." Because God's Word says if we resist the enemy, he'll flee from us (James 4:7). Once you recognize such thoughts as the voice of Satan, you can just brush them aside. "I refuse to listen to you anymore. I'm not going to listen to a liar, a deceiver, and a cheat. That's not true. Those are lies (or exaggerations, misinterpretations, half–truths, etc.)." Just fight the devil positively when he tries to make you bitter or upset at others or at the Lord. Start singing a hymn or song to Jesus. Pray and quote the Word of God. Just let the Light in and the darkness flees every time. When you're being tempted or attacked with negative or critical thoughts, you just have to be positive and attack back. You have to make a conscious effort to rebuke the devil and think positive, and good thoughts instead. If you watch your thoughts and words, fill your heart and mind with the Lord and His Word, you will be well–protected, fortified, and surrounded by God's angels of protection. You will be free from the enemy's critical and confusing static, negative accusations, and doubts. In whatever you might do in every activity of life and everything you do or say or even think, ask the Lord to help you to be constantly on guard. You can monitor your thoughts, monitor your words, and monitor your actions just like we monitor videos. Then you can always choose the good and eschew the evil. "Let love be without dissimulation [hypocrisy] Abhor that which is evil; cleave to that which is good" (Romans 12:9). Paul tells us to let our love be genuine for one another and when something evil appears, get away from it. This will be dangerous in your walk with God. "Let this mind be in you which was also in Christ Jesus" (Philippians 2:5). This verse in the amplified version is stated this way: "Let this same attitude and purpose and humble mind be in you which was in Christ Jesus. Let him be your example in humility." What kind of mind did Christ have? He made himself no reputation. He took on the form of a servant. He fashioned himself like a man. He humbled himself and became obedient even unto the death of the cross. When he had finished doing all of this, the Bible says God highly exalted him, gave him a name above every name. Everything will have to bow to that name Jesus, the things in the earth, things in heaven, and things under the earth; and every tongue will confess that Jesus is Lord. "I can do all things through Christ which strengtheneth me" (Philippians 4:12). When we look into where the Apostle Paul was when he wrote this letter, it gives us an insight into his thought pattern. Even though he is sitting in a Roman jail cell, his mind is not in a jail cell. It reminds me of a story that I heard a Baptist preacher say. There was a little girl with her mom in the car, this little girl would not be still and kept moving around. Her mom would tell her over and over, "Sit down please." After about the fifth or sixth time, the mom stopped the car and put her in a seatbelt. The mom started riding and looked over at the little girl, and she was just smiling. Her mom asked her, "Why are you smiling so much?" The little girl answered her, "Mom, I might be in this seatbelt, but my mind is still playing." That is what Apostle Paul was saying. "My body is in this jail, but my mind is in Philippi." That is the same way with us. We might be going through something, but our minds are free to live this life God gave us through his Son.

GUARDING YOUR SPIRIT AGAINST OFFENCES

In order for us to deal with this chapter, we must first define what an offense is. The word *offense* comes from the Greek word *skandalon*, "to scandalize, a stumbling block, a displeasing taste, to cause resentment and anger." We must guard our hearts, minds, and spirits so these things don't destroy us. Jesus said in the book of St. Luke 17:1, "It is impossible but that offenses will come: but woe unto him, through whom they come." The Amplified Bible says it this way: "Temptations, snares, traps set entice to sin are sure to come, but woe to him by or through whom they come." When I read this scripture about Jesus giving us knowledge about offenses, it helps me realize that I cannot live in this world without becoming offended. The thing that is important to me and my relationship with God is how I choose to handle the offense and the offender. Let us look at the life of another man in the Bible who did not handle his offence in the right spirit. "And Absalom sent for Ahithophel the Gilonite, David's counselor, from his city, even from Giloh, while he offered sacrifices. And the conspiracy was strong; for the people increased continually with Absalom" (2 Samuel 15:12). Who is this man Ahithoplel? He was one of King David's best counselors. He was also the grandfather of Bathsheba and the father of Eliam. This is one reason Ahithophel turned against David. The bitterness built within his heart for years until there was a time when he found somebody with a grudge against David also. He found a good candidate. David's son Absalom. The Bible tells us that the conspiracy was strong because David realized how powerful the counsel of Ahithophel was. "And one told David, saying 'Ahithophel is among the conspirators with Absalom.' And David said, 'O Lord, I pray thee turn the counsel of Ahithophel into foolishness'" (2 Samuel 16:31). Why would David give such a response to the information about Ahithophel? One reason David knew the counsel of this man, that if he said something, it was like God himself said it. "And the counsel of Ahithophel, which he counseled in those days, was as if a man had inquired at the oracle of God: so was the counsel of Ahithophel with David and Absalom" (2 Samuel 16:23). The counsel of Ahithophel to Absalom was given out of the hatred and bitterness that Ahithophel had allowed to build up in his heart. The counsel was given first to disgrace King David, and the second part of the counsel was given to defeat King David (2 Samuel 16:20–23). He tells Absalom to take his father's concubines and lay with them on top of the roof of the palace. This act disgraces King David and makes the problem worst between father and son, which would never heal. The next counsel Ahithophel gave was to get an army of twelve thousand men and pursue David until he is weary, weakened, and afraid. The counsel of Ahithophel pleased Absalom. If Absalom would have followed the second part of Ahithophel's counsel, David would have been defeated; but God had another plan. A young man by the name of Hushai, who was David's trusted friend, became a spy in the camp of Absalom and contradicted all the counsel of Ahithophel. (Second Samuel 17:23) gives us the tragic end of this man who had great wisdom until he allowed bitterness to take over his life: "When Ahithophel saw that his counsel had been rejected, he went home and set his house in order and then hanged himself and died."

When we failed to release the hurt, pain, and anger of the offence, this keeps us from being effective and fruitful in the kingdom of God and effective in our spiritual lives. "For by thy words thou shalt be justified and by thy words shalt be condemned. Dealing with the spirit of offence is definitely a matter of the heart" (Matthew 12:37). To be offended or to experience offence is not a pleasurable feeling; but instead of us facing and dealing with the emotions of being offended, we allow them to grow into bitterness and resentment that, in the long run of life, will damage our character and affect our ability to love as God told us to love thy brother. When we allow the spirit of bitterness to enter into our minds, we enter into a spiritual warfare on another level. In Philippians 4:8. Paul tells us the things we should be thinking on: the things that are honest, the things that are pure, the things that are just, the things that are lovely, things of good report. If there be any virtue or things that are praiseworthy, think on these things. We, as Christians, must realize that the only power the enemy has is the power of suggestion and influence. We must not allow the enemy to gain control of our minds. I have come to learn that to deny that something has happened does not mean I am delivered from that situation, so we must come out of denial and be honest with ourselves. God will not deal with anything we are not willing to face. When we are hurt or when we hurt someone, let us be honest and repent so we can be free to worship God as our savior.

The Bible also says offence must come. Given this piece of knowledge, it is impossible to believe that we will live in this world without becoming offended. The important thing to do when an offence comes is to guard your heart, mind, and spirit. The failure to release the hurt, pain, and anger the offence might have brought to your heart, mind, and spirit will cause you to become ineffective and uncaring in your Christian walk.

Out of the heart the mouth speaks. Dealing with offence is definitely a matter of the heart. In order for someone to have the ability to offend you, there must be a level of respect, love, and trust for him/her. Being offended or experiencing offence is not a pleasurable emotion. Many of us allow those feelings of hurt to develop into bitterness and resentment. It is important that we do not allow those hurts to define our character and affect our ability to love. Bitterness harbored in our hearts will cause us to disconnect from the people we love, organizations we have devoted our life work to, and from anything that has the potential to cause us pain again. God is love.

Since God is love, Christians must always be a living, breathing being demonstrating the power of His love. Instead of allowing the spirit of offence to take root in our heart and create grudges, we should overlook the issue that caused the offence and forgive. Forgiving a person does not mean that you forget what a person has done. Forgiveness means you no longer allow what has happened to affect your actions, attitude, and frame of mind. The inability to forgive stops God's plan for our life. God's says if we do not forgive, we will not be forgiven. The ability to forgive allows God's grace to rest, rule, and abide in our lives. We need to realize there are going to be times when we are going to offend someone, intentionally or unintentionally, because we are imperfect people, since we are guilty of being an offender. We must quickly forgive and repent so that nothing enters our hearts. The golden rule is to treat others the way we want to be treated. So it is vital that we set an example of God's grace, love, kindness, and forgiveness when it comes to dealing with people who have offended us. Don't accept those things in your hearts, in your relationships, or in your house. Kick them out.

Secondly, perception is everything when it comes to dealing with the spirit of offence. When we allow the spirit of offence to enter into our mind, we enter into spiritual warfare on a higher level. Philippians 4:8 tells us to dwell; ponder; think; consider; keep our mind on things that are honest, just, pure, lovely, of a good report, and if there be any virtue or things that are praiseworthy, to think on those things. If we are battling with the spirit of offence, we are pondering and thinking on the thing that caused us pain, hurt, anger, and disappointment. The only power the devil has is the power of suggestion and of influence. As Christians, we cannot give him the power to rule our mind.

When it comes to issues related to the mind, we must first come out of denial and be honest. If someone has hurt, offended, or disappointed us, we must admit it to ourselves, to the person who offended us, and to God. God will not deal with anything we are not willing to recognize. The admission of hurt will hinder the endless flow of thoughts that contain bitterness, anger, and unforgivness. Secondly, we cannot think too much on the offence. An idle mind is the devil's workshop. When thoughts of the offence enter into our minds, we must wash our thoughts with his Word. By applying God's Word to any situation or circumstance, it counteracts any subtle thought the enemy would like to plant in our mind. Lastly, we must seek a solution and make peace with the final solution. The person who offended us will not always give an apology and be remorseful because of the hurt, but we must be able to accept what that person's response is and move on.

"The spirit of a man will sustain his infirmity, but a wounded spirit who can bear?" (Proverbs 18:14). If we choose to focus on an offence, it will continue to wound our spirit. It will cause us to display unreasonable, anger-filled actions and unbearable attitudes. Failing to guard our spirit from offences will allow our inner man to become preoccupied with past hurts. Offended people can turn kind actions of others into additional grievances and another source for offences to grow from.

GETTING TO THE ROOT

I am not much of a person who plants gardens or flowers, or anything of that nature. I can look at them real hard and they will die, but there is one thing I have learned about gardening. If you don't get to the root of something, it will not die. You can cut it off on the surface but if you don't get to the very thing that gives it life, it will only grow back again. I must admit it takes a whole lot of work to get to the root of something, but it is well worth it when you finish so other plants will not be destroyed because you allowed a root of something deadly to stay in the ground. There is a flower that grows in the yard of many people that is called poison ivy. This plant is known for the poison that flows from it. The fluid that comes out of it affects the skin with whelps, bumps, and itching; and the infection has been known to get in the blood. There are some people so allergic to this plant for them even being around it, affects them. Bitterness is like this plant; it is poison and will affect the people around you. In the book of Hebrews, it talks about a root of bitterness that will destroy and trouble you. It is called a root of bitterness because like roots of a plant are hidden beneath the ground and grow downward in the soil, so does the root of bitterness in the soil of our hearts. Just as roots of plants and trees wrap around other things underground, the same will happen to our hearts if we do not get the root of bitterness out. I remember a few years ago the pipes of our church clogged up. We did everything humanly possible to unstop those pipes. We would go a week or two, and we thought we had it. When we looked around again, the toilets were overflowing and backing up again. Finally, we brought in a plumber. He had to dig up the concrete walkway; and about fifteen feet from the church, what we found was amazing. The roots of the trees and hedges had grown through the pipes and clogged them up. I asked the plumber, "How did these roots grow through these pipes like that?" His response was shocking, and he said that roots will follow water in order to nourish themselves. I thought about the heart that has a root of bitterness in it. That same heart will follow hurt, rebellion, family traits, deceit, hatred, rejection, jealousy, envy, and many other things that will dominate their lives. "Looking diligently lest any man fail of the grace of God; lest a root of bitterness springing up trouble you, and thereby many be defiled" (Hebrews 12:15). The Message Bible quotes this verse like this: "Keep a sharp eye out for weeds of bitter discontent. A thistle or two gone to seed can ruin the whole garden in no time." This verse gives us the devastating effect that bitterness has on us as the people of God. It will cause us to not enjoy the grace that God gave us through his Son, Jesus Christ. The next part of the verse says it will trouble you, which simply means it will cause relationships to be damaged or even destroyed. The bitterness I carry will destroy the lives of people around me. Bitterness will also affect our health, both physically and spiritually. "Follow peace with all men and holiness, without which no man shall see the Lord" (Hebrews 12:14). God, through Jesus Christ, has given a life of peace to enjoy; but when we hold to bitterness, we forfeit that joy.

> These things have I spoken unto you, that my joy might remain in you, and that your joy might be full. This verse says this in the Message Bible, I've told you these things for a pur-

> pose: that my joy might be your joy, and your joy wholly mature.
>
> St. John 15:11

Jesus gave us this verse so we can understand that it is His will that we enjoy life to the fullest. We are able to experience the fullest of joy by remaining in fellowship with Him through all the tests of life.

The spirit of bitterness has the ability to infiltrate and influence every area and aspect of our Christian life. In order to prevent this invasion, we must choose to get to the root of the bitterness and uproot that source of pain out of out of our minds, hearts, and spirits. The uprooting of bitterness is not an easy process, but it requires a clear and concise plan of action. Once a plan of action has been developed, believers must do their due diligence to execute the plan and begin to enjoy a prosperous and successful spirit–filled life.

There is a saying: "Admitting you have a problem is the first step to recovery." Living in a state of denial for a Christian is a dangerous thing. The spirit of denial gives saints a false sense of security, growth, and deliverance. Denial will cause believers to scheme and manipulate a plan of evil and retribution for the people perceived as doing them wrong. As believers, we must admit if the spirit of bitterness is operating in our lives. The admission of this spirit operating must be made to ourselves and to God. Oftentimes, our pride keeps us from admitting we are bitter about our circumstances, situations, experiences, and positions in life. The confession of bitterness and pride in our lives will open the door for God to come in and deal with the root of problem and the source of the bitterness. Not only will God begin to deal with our issues but He will heal us from the matters. Admitting that bitterness has taken root in our lives will also help Christians place things into perspective. When God begins to deal with the source of our bitterness, it's important to write things down or think the problem through. By writing things down or thinking things through, we are able to process the feelings associated with the offence that created bitterness.

Following the admission of possessing a spirit of bitterness, believers must pray for forgiveness. But the prayer for forgiveness must be a three–fold prayer. First, Christians must ask God to forgive them of the bitterness they have toward the person or the people whom they have bitterness toward. Harboring bitterness in our life is a sin. The Bible clearly lets us know that a sinner will not tarry in His sight, so repentance and seeking forgiveness from God is key when moving forth in God.

In conjunction with asking God for forgiveness, it is necessary to ask God to show us how he can use the people, circumstances, and incidents as a tool to mold us into better people. It is critical to realize that God allowed these events to occur in our lives. This is not to say that God caused it, but He did allow it. Nothing in life happens by chance, but it is orchestrated by the hand of God.

Besides asking God for forgiveness, it is vital to ask the people who know you were acting in a spirit of bitterness for forgiveness also. Operating in a spirit of bitterness affects relationships. Bitterness causes the lines of communication to shut down. Where there is no communication, walls begin to develop, homes fall apart, and the spirit man begins to dwindle. Holding bitterness toward someone will prevent the love of God from following, and it hardens the hearts of all. Asking people for forgiveness isn't going to heal the relationships overnight, but it starts the healing process. It is going to take time to really deal with matters that caused the bitterness, but it is another point of entrance for God to begin uprooting bitterness out of the believers' life.

Lastly, the person harboring bitterness must pray for a spirit of release from the bitterness. While releasing the bitterness and seeking forgiveness from all parties are great starting points, it is important to realize that it's not always possible to forget what happened. Releasing the bitterness simply means to cease from feeling resentment against someone or something. Releasing bitterness over the issue will take the power from the source of the incident or the person that caused bitterness in the believers' life. God wants Christians to be able to endure many tests, storms, and trials. After enduring all those things God wants Christians to live a life that does not have any residue or painleft behind from those unpleasant incidents in life.

No matter how valid the issues are that planted the seed of bitterness in a believers' heart, there comes a time when believers need to get over the bitterness and let it go. The first and most important obstacle to overcome is to acknowledge that bitterness exists in some form in our Christian life. Failure to acknowledge the bitterness will create feelings of anger, hurt, frustration, and irritation. These emotions are not godly and will cause Christians to act out of character and nature. Those underlying emotions will not allow God to uproot the bitterness; will allow the bitterness to take a firmer and deeper root in our lives, hearts, minds, and spirits. Secondly, we must ask for forgiveness and forgive. Forgiveness is God's answer to life's unexpected disappointments, hurts, and misunderstandings. The ability to forgive and ask for forgiveness will allow God to come in and show His grace in every area of our life. It will also humble all parties in the circumstance that was the source of the bitterness. Lastly, bitterness must be released. Releasing bitterness will free Christians' minds, souls, hearts, and spirits. Moving on from a bitter incident will make believers more effective vessels for the Master's use. We must realize that God brought the incident our way as a learning tool for us to grow from.

THE EFFECTS OF BITTERNESS

How can one's individual bitterness defile many? Well, there are several ways a person's bitterness can spoil into the lives of many and affect a multitude. For one thing, people who are really bitter about one thing will easily become bitter about other things too. Bitterness will cause a person to find a problem or make an issue out of something very small simply because they have an issue. The need to find fault or error usually comes from the need to place blame on someone. Bitter people typically believe they are never wrong. Bitterness will cause people to become self–righteous hypocrites, who will never know the joy of really knowing what true love, peace, and the fullness of life really is.

Bitterness is a root for people to become antisocial. Bitter people are discontented, resentful, and critical.

They are usually never satisfied unless they can persuade others to agree with their opinion. Misery loves company, and they love to have other people agree with them. It's sad to say, but it's usually easy to find them. Bellyaching, murmuring, and complaining is a very common ailment of the human race and something that is very easy to fall into. But from God's point of view, it is a sin that is absolutely intolerable. Just read the story of the wandering children of Israel and you'll see how He let millions of people wander in the Sinaitic Desert for their murmuring and their complaining, and they never got into the Promised Land (Numbers 32:11–13). Bitterness and murmuring are a very infectious spiritual disease, diabolical, and can spread and poison others very quickly if left unchecked. One bad apple can do it so fast. The Bible warns us, "Know ye not that a little leaven leaveneth the whole lump? Purge out therefore the old leaven, that ye may be a new lump" (1Corinthians 5:6,–7). Just like a tiny pinch of yeast will spread throughout an entire lump of dough and cause the whole thing to rise, people who are permeated with bitterness are a real burden, a downer, and a negative influence. They can pull everybody's spirits down. They're always dwelling on the negative, always criticizing and murmuring. Bitter people are selfish, inconsiderate of others, withdrawn from society, indifferent, adverse to conformity with conventional standards, norms, and social behaviors.

HOW BITTERNESS AFFECTS YOUR HEALTH

The affairs of the heart and affairs of the spirit can affect you physically. In medical science, they call such afflictions psychosomatic illnesses, which means they are caused by your mind. But we'd say they're caused by your spirit, by an improper attitude of heart, primarily a lack of love for the Lord and others. There are all kinds of little roots: little roots of bitterness, little roots of jealousy, little roots of resentment, and little roots of hurt feelings. They can all get bitter, grow, and begin to eat away at you from within. If you let those seeds of bitterness grow, there will be obvious manifestations in all areas of your life. Doctors have found that people who are bitter and have a lot of hatred in their hearts have much more arthritis than those who are at peace. Similarly, they've discovered that those who have a lot of fear in their minds—worries, tension, phobias, etc.—have a lot more mental trouble and more stomach trouble as well as more heart trouble. Thank God that the elimination of fear by faith gives peace of mind, rest to your stomach, rest to your heart, and eliminates various poisons that cause illness from the blood. In other words, your state of mind and heart can actually poison your body. Science knows this and has proven it true.

As mentioned before, our bodies eventually break down from stress. Strife brings stress, and stress brings sickness. Many families are also experiencing financial pressure, which brings on stress. Tired people succumb to temptation easier than rested ones. Tired people get angry quicker. They are more impatient and more easily frustrated. It doesn't take a genius to recognize the plan of Satan. Being under constant stress will make you sick.

Each time you get upset, your emotions rise to the boiling point, causing the internal organs to work harder to accommodate the strain. They will only last for a certain period of time; and then they begin to wear out, showing signs of the strain they have been under. Let me share with you what your body goes through internally each time you get upset. "Although I am not a doctor," says Joyce Meyers, author of *Life*

Without Stress, "but in my own terms, I will try to explain what happens. The onset of stress sets off an alarm in our body to defend itself from threatening events. Even thinking of an upsetting event or imaging danger can set off the alarm. A chain of internal responses are set into motion, and we are prepared to fight the danger or run from it. This is called fight or flight. The stressor (the thing that is causing stress) sends a message to your brain through the pituitary gland and nervous system. Your brain sends the alarm message to your adrenal gland, which releases hormones such as adrenaline increasing your heart rate, raising cholesterol. The threat of stress sets in motion a complex chain of responses, to prepare us for fight or flight, whether to attack what is threatening us or to run away from it. The body says to the organs, 'I am under attack. Help me fight this, or help me to get away from it. I need extra strength and energy to help me in this emergency.' The body organs begin to help. They are equipped to handle emergencies, but when a person lives in a perpetual state of emergencies, the organs wear out. The time comes when the organs are extremely worn out and they find they can no longer handle normal stress. Suddenly something snaps. For some people it is their minds. For others it's their emotions, for many others, their physical heath is affected."

Here is an example of what happens. Take a rubber band, and stretch it out as far as you can. Then let it relax. Do this over and over. After a while, you will find that the rubber band loses it elasticity. It becomes limp. Keep the process up long enough and finally, one stretch too many, it snaps. This is what happens to us if we keep stretching ourselves too far too many times.

Finally, sickness arrives. People say, "I don't know what is wrong, but I just don't feel good." They have headaches, backaches, neck and shoulder pain, strain, stomach ulcers, colon problems, and other ailments. They tell the doctor how they feel. He calls it adrenal weakness, a virus, or something else.

In many instances, the root cause is years of strife-filled, stressful living. Stress causes illness by destroying the body's immunological defense system. The individual's body cannot fight off germs and infections. The organs just plain wear out. The individual feels exhausted.

Negative words and thoughts can cause stress, and stress can cause sickness. Positive thoughts, words, and emotions bring heath and healing. Consider the following five scriptures.

"A calm and undisturbed mind and heart are the life and health of the body, but envy, jealousy, and wrath are like rottenness of the bones" (Proverbs 14:30).

Wrath is violent, resentful anger or rage. To be wrathful means to be very angry. Such upset causes sickness because the emotional turmoil eats away at good health and a sound body. A calm and peaceful mind ministers health to the entire being.

"My son, attend to my words consent and submit to my sayings. Let them not depart from your sight. Keep them in the center of your heart. For they are life to those who find them, healing and health to all your flesh"

Proverbs 4–20–22.

What brings and ministers healing and heath? Mediating on God's Word and not on the things that causes stress. Jesus is our peace. He is also the living Word. When we aide in the Word, peace is abundant. It flows like a river.

"Lean on, trust in, and be confident in the Lord with all your heart and mind and do not rely on your own understanding. In all your ways know recognize, and acknowledge Him, and He will direct and make straight and plain your paths. Be not wise in your own eyes, reverently fear and worship the Lord and turn (entirely) away from evil. It shall be health to your nerves and sinews and marrow and moistening to your bones."

Proverbs 3:5–6.

When the mind is calm, our health is protected. The wise man trusts in God rather than worrying. Joyce Myers said that she spent many years reasoning and trying to figure everything out and it affected her health adversely. She feels much better physically now than she did when she was thirty–five. Why? Because she doesn't worry now. She has learned to cast her cares upon God so that she doesn't live under constant pressure. "There are those who speak rashly, like the piercing of a sword, but the tongue of the wise brings healing"

Proverbs 12:18.

Speaking rashly often starts arguments. The phrase "piercing of a sword" is descriptive of hurtful words that stab and wound. But a wise man can use his mouth to bring healing. Have your mouth full of the Word of God, not your own words. Your health will improve.

"A happy heart is good medicine and a cheerful mind works healing but a broken spirit dries up the bones"

Proverbs 17:22.

How much plainer could it be said? A person who is happy, lighthearted, and cheerful will be healthy. An angry person is neither cheerful nor happy and very likely not healthy either. Jesus gave us the answer to life's potential stressors. He said, "I want you to have perfect peace and confidence. In the world you will have tribulation and trails and distress and frustrations. But be of good cheer. For I have overcome the world. I have deprived it of power to harm you and have conquered it for you"

John 16:33.

HOW BITTERNESS AFFECTS YOUR SPIRIT

When we're attacking the enemy and doing all we can to conquer new territory and win new souls for God's kingdom, the devil, of course, is going to be quite busy trying to *stop* us. While the devil is out to stop us, it is necessary to thank God because the only way he, the devil, can stop us is if we allow him to. But if, in some way, you are harboring his negative and destructive thoughts, listening to his debilitating doubts, or entertaining his faith weakening fears, that is a partial *surrender* to the enemy. And any surrender to the devil is always going to cause you *trouble*. If you allow bitterness and resentment and a critical spirit to grow in your life, you will lose your anointing and your inspiration from the Lord. You can't keep complaining about and resenting your lot in life and criticizing and murmuring about things that God or others have done to you, and keep God's Holy Spirit on you at the same time. You just can't do it. The Lord dwells in the *praises* of His people, and He draws near to *us* when we draw near to *Him*. "Offering the sacrifice of *praise* to God continually, that is, the fruit of our lips giving *thanks* to His name" (Psalm 22:3, James 4:8, Hebrews 13:15). "But without *faith* it is *impossible* to please Him" (Hebrews 11:6). If you don't accept the things that the Lord sends into your life, if you not only doubt and wonder about His treatment and care of you but actually murmur and resent and rebel against it, that's certainly not faith and surely displeases the Lord. And if you allow that root of bitterness to take hold in your heart and life, it will cause you to fail both the Lord and yourself. Such a root can go a hell of a long way and can ultimately destroy you. It can at least destroy your ministry and your effectiveness for the Lord, and it can even harm the entire work of God that you're supposed to be helping. The way that bitterness can hinder your ministry and effectiveness is illustrated in the following true story about the great artist and engineer Leonardo da Vinci. Just before he commenced work on his famous painting of *The Last Supper*, he had a violent quarrel with a fellow painter. He was so enraged and bitter that he decided to paint the face of his enemy, the other artist, into the face of Judas and thus take his revenge by handing the man down in infamy and scorn to succeeding generations. The face of Judas was therefore one of the first that he finished, and everyone could easily recognize it as the face of the painter with whom da Vinci had quarreled. But when he came to paint the face of Jesus, he could make no progress. Something seemed to be baffling him, holding him back and frustrating his best efforts. At length, he came to the conclusion that the thing that was checking and frustrating him was the fact that he had painted his enemy into the face of Judas. He therefore painted out the face of Judas and commenced anew on the face of Jesus, this time with the success that the ages have acclaimed. How clearly this incident shows us that we cannot, at one and the same time, be painting the features of Christ into our own life and be painting another face with the colors of enmity and hatred. To become more Christlike and to accomplish what the Lord wants you to do, surely all bitterness and hatred must be put away and laid aside.

THE HEALING POWER OF FORGIVENESS

There is an old saying, that forgiveness is the key that unlocks the door to resentment and the handcuffs of hate. It is the power that breaks the chains of bitterness and the shackles of selfishness. The Lord and His love, mercy, and forgiveness are the antidote for the deadly poison of bitterness. A little love can go such a long way and no matter what the problems is or where the root of bitterness might have stemmed from, love can still cover a multitude of sin on the part of whoever is to blame. Even if you don't understand exactly what the problem is between you and someone else, the Lord understands and the answer is love. "Love never fails" (1 Corinthians 13:8). Past differences, hurts, and grievances can all be healed through humility, love, and the oil of the Spirit. In my research, I found statements made by Archbishop Desmond Tutu, a leader in Africa during the time of apartheid, that shed some much needed light on the subject of bitterness. He was asked a question by a reporter about how he would handle all of the awful things that had happened to him and people he knew. He answered, "Without forgiveness there is no future, without forgiveness there is no freedom, without forgiveness there is no recovery, and without forgiveness there is no healing." If we could keep this in our mind when bad things happen to us, we can handle it better. The next statement I found was made by Daddy King, the father of Dr. Martin Luther King, Jr. In 1968, he had to deal with seeing his son Martin, Jr., assassinated, his second son drowned in a backyard pool in 1969, and in 1974, he saw the woman he loved and the mother of his children murdered by a man in the congregation, who shot her while she was playing the organ. Daddy King was asked, "How do you handle all of the bad things that have taken place with your family?" Daddy King replied, "There is no time for hate and no reason for it, nothing that a man does takes him lower than when he allows himself to fall so low as to hate someone. To hate is to live in the past, to dwell on deeds that already happen." This is very true, I have learned. I must be honest. I'm still learning that it is much more difficult to hate than to love. "Only by pride cometh contention" (Proverbs 13:10). Love, humility, and prayer solve all problems. It never fails. Love casts a veil over countless sins. Love can cover all of the past sins and mistakes that you or whoever you're having problems with have made. The divine, supernatural, miraculous, infinite, marvelous love of God is love enough to forgive. In fact, if you don't have love enough to forgive, you don't have love because forgiveness is love. So if you can't forgive, you cannot possibly have real love or real humility. You do not have mercy because love is forgiveness and mercy. As we've already pointed out, it's all too easy for us to go down the line and blame others for everything that's wrong with us and for all our problems. "Oh, they mistreated me and weren't fair to me." "They didn't keep me in line and they didn't help me to do what is right." They let me do the wrong thing." But when we forgive others, we no longer blame them. Once bitterness has had the opportunity to grow in your heart, it's very easy to become very unloving and hard toward those you feel bitter against. Your spirit can then be very unforgiving, intolerant, and impatient, if you are living in a state of bitterness. Instead of making it easier for others, you make it harder for them by reacting in a judging and critical spirit, hard heart, self-righteous and unforgiving attitude. If you've been this way, you'd better ask those toward whom you've been bitter to forgive you for your unloving, critical spirit and receive them with wide-open arms. If you want to forsake and get rid of your bitterness, you have to forgive. If you truly forgive someone, that means you let go of whatever it is you're harboring in your heart against them. You can't say you forgive, but can never forget. That statement simply means you're still holding it against them. Those who say they will forgive but not forget are all too often simply burying the hatchet, but leaving the handle out for future use. When you've had a problem with bitterness, you've got to be willing to absolutely release and forsake all of your past bitterness and grievances toward others. You've got to "forget those things which are behind, and reach forth unto those things which are before" (Philippians 3:13). Here's how one author accurately described bitterness and forgiveness:

> Carrying a grudge is a loser's game. It is the ultimate frustration because it leaves you with more pain than you had in the first place. Recall the pain of being wronged, the hurt of being stung, cheated, and demeaned. Doesn't the memory of it fuel the fire of fury again? Do you feel

> that hurt each time your memory lights on the people who did you wrong? Your own memory becomes a videotape within your soul that plays unending reruns of your old rendezvous with pain. Is this fair to yourself—this wretched justice of not forgiving? The only way to heal the pain that will not heal itself is to forgive the person who hurt you. Forgiving heals your memory as you change your memory's vision. When you release the wrongdoer from the wrong, you cut a malignant tumor out of your inner life. You set a prisoner free: yourself.
>
> Lewis B. Smedes

The Lord commands us to forgive those who have trespassed against us and that means we can no longer blame them. Even if they were initially responsible for troubling us or causing us to have problems, we cannot continue to blame them for our problems, if we truly forgive them. If we have problems that resulted from others mistreating us, and those problems continue, it's our fault because the Lord has given us the power to overcome these things. The Lord wants us to forgive those people and ask Him for His deliverance from those problems; so we can overcome them and be free from their hindrance. The Lord wants us to take the responsibility for our part in the problem.

By accepting our part he is able to show His power and His deliverance. God wants us to know that no matter what has happened to us in the past, it doesn't have to affect our whole lives. We don't have to carry that load with us for the rest of our lives. The Word says, "Every man shall give an account of himself unto God" (Romans 14:12). But if you don't accept the responsibility for your present problems and quit blaming them on others, you're going to wind up going through your entire life never getting the victory or making any progress spiritually. How can you possibly grow and learn any lessons if you self–righteously blame other people for everything bad that's ever happened to you? If you hang onto your bitterness and refuse to forgive others, then the Lord cannot forgive you or help you very much. Jesus said, "If ye forgive men their trespasses, your Heavenly Father will also forgive you. But if ye forgive not men their trespasses, neither will your Heavenly Father forgive your trespasses" (Matthew 6:14–15). The Lord is able and willing to help you truly forgive others. He will help you get rid of that bitterness if you sincerely ask Him and are willing to genuinely let go of every grudge, thought, or resentment you might be clinging to. If you've had a part in any past wrongdoings you might have suffered, you've got to be honest and confess it, so that the Lord can heal deliver, and forgive you. His Word says, "If we confess our sins, He is faithful and just to forgive us our sins" (1 John 1:9). But if we don't even confess our sins, if we don't even think something's are our fault, then how can the Lord forgive us? Even if we were entirely guiltless in the wrongs done to us in the past, we are guilty in that we become bitter about it. If we blame someone else for our present problems because of some wrong they did to us in the past, we are wrong. Our present problems are our fault. If your desire is to truly love, serve, and worship the Lord "in spirit and in truth" (John 4:24), then you've got to get rid of that heavy burden of bitterness and blame that you are carrying around and putting on other people for your problems. Failure to release the burdens will cause you to never be able to accomplish much for the Lord. Blaming others for your present problems is just murmuring and complaining. You are responsible for what you do from now on. Are you blaming your problems on others? Have you forgiven from your heart those who have hurt you in the past? Or are you using that as an excuse for your present problems? Remember, "Every one of us shall give an account of himself to God" (Romans 14:12). You are responsible for your own actions. So for God's sake, forgive those who have trespassed against you, so the Lord can forgive you for your trespasses. "Forget those things which are behind and reach forth unto the things which are before, and press towards the mark for the prize of the high calling of God in Christ Jesus" (Philippians 3:13–14).When you're determined to utterly forsake a spiritual problem like bitterness and you call out to the Lord with a whole heart, asking Him to deliver you, it only takes one blast of the mighty searing power of the Holy Ghost to burn out all the devil's old circuits in a mighty infilling of God's Spirit, God's great electrical power. When you sincerely call out to the Lord to deliver you, He does His part and will fulfill His promise: "A new heart will I give you, and a new spirit will I put within you" (Ezekiel 36:26). But even though you are a new creature, that old self will still try to pop up again. You have to fight the devil, your old self, and your old bad habits every day. So be prepared for a battle every day, especially with your besetting sins, "the weights and sins that do so easily beset you" (Hebrews 12:1). The Lord will be faithful to answer prayer and do His part. But then you've got to do your part by exerting the effort to forsake and "put off" all of the old negative thought patterns and bad habits. His Word says:

> That ye put off concerning the former conversation the old man, which is corrupt according to the deceitful lusts; And be renewed in the spirit of your mind; And that ye put on the new man, which after God is created in righteousness and true holiness.
>
> Ephesians 4:22–24

You need to really give the Lord a lot of cooperation in working on breaking any bad habits of bitterness you've formed. You need to ask Him to change your entire outlook and attitude toward those whom you've been bitter against. You don't always necessarily get over this sort of thing in a day. It might sometimes take a little while. The enemy doesn't easily yield territory that he's controlled. When people have had weaknesses and channels open to the enemy before, he'll try to get that ground back if he can. So you've got to keep praying that the Lord will deliver you and give you the complete victory, rewire you completely. You have to be absolutely rewired and have your mind transformed by the Spirit of God, and it usually takes time to rewire or reprogram a computer. Any psychologist will tell you that a new thought pattern cannot be established until the old one has had time to be completely erased—in your case, only by a miracle of God. Ask Him to put a new mind in you, "That mind which is in Christ Jesus" (Philippians 2:5). That takes a genuine spiritual renewal, a real rewiring of all the nerves and nerve centers and mental facilities, to make sure the Lord has complete control and the devil's previous channels are broken completely.

If you have to fight a real big battle to get the victory, the Lord will give you a lot more credit and a lot more reward. If you have a real tough battle and struggle to get the victory, it's probably because the Lord's testing you to find out how much you want it and how much you're willing to fight for it before He's going to reward you with it. But if you do your part, the Lord will certainly do His part and you will win. So don't give up. Praise the Lord.

MY STORY

There might be many people wondering or saying to themselves, how can you write a book on such a topic as bitterness? As the topic of this chapter will lead you to believe, bitterness was an issue I had to battle with a lot in my life; and it's my story. I had a wonderful childhood. God blessed me with great parents; but like many of the families in the world today, we had our fair share of family issues. I believe from the fall of Adam and Eve that every family after that is living with some type of dysfunction. My family was no different.

My father and mother were married for almost forty–three years. They had their ups and downs like every married couple, but they raised the seven of us in a home that was filled with love and a strong dose of reality. I am truly grateful for the way my parents raised my siblings and I. The only commandment of the Ten Commandments that comes with a promise attached to it tells us to honor our father and mother that our days may be long upon the land. God tells us, "Honor thy father and thy mother that thy days may be long upon the land which the Lord thy God giveth thee" (Exodus 20:12). My grandmother used to drill this verse into my mind. Her purpose for this constant reminder was to ensure that I would always respect my mom and dad. Showing respect for my parents was hard to do at times. The inability to show respect was due to some of the things I had to put up with and learn to accept when I should have been enjoying being a child. Around the age of twelve, things in our family began to change drastically. My father began to sell alcohol from our home. The selling and use of alcohol became a sedative for my mom. She began to drown her hurts and problems with alcohol. This newfound sedative became a twelve–year addiction. This addiction disrupted our whole family. I am not saying my father did not have any issues. My father's issues did not spawn the abuse and chaos that drinking brought into our home. He was never a drinker, but he worked all the time. He gambled and loved his share of his women. I often tell people that children who are raised up in alcoholic homes, drug–abuse homes, or a physically abusive home have to deal with many dramatic hurts and devastating pains.

There were seven children in our family. There were six boys and one girl. It seemed to me that my sister and I caught the backlash of all my mother's bitterness. My sister was the main receipiant of my mom's anger and bitterness. She was the only girl. My mom did not want a daughter. She would often remind my sister of that fact when she was drinking.

At an early age, I joined the work force. I would go to the golf course and worked as caddy. I would do this all day sometimes to earn a little money as a young man. Having this job initially was a blessing, but it soon became a curse too. My mom would beat me with anything she could get her hands on if I did not give her the money. I would work so hard in the summer sun until my clothes were filled with sweat just for her to get another drink. The ironic thing about my mom and her drinking was no one ever knew when the drinking would start and when it would end. A great indicator that she had been drinking was when we approached the house and every word spoken was cursing, hollering, or screaming at us. This lifestyle went on for twelve years.

At the age of thirteen or fourteen, I began smoking cigarettes, drinking, and using drugs. My life was on a crash course for about six to seven years. This fast–living and sin–filled life stopped when I met a young lady at the age of nineteen, who introduced me to Jesus Christ and turned my whole life around. I married this same woman, who became the love of my life. This year, we will celebrate thirty–seven years of marriage. Through meeting this great woman of God and her introducing me to Jesus Christ, my whole life changed. "Therefore if any man be in Christ he is a new creature; old things are passed away; behold all things become new" (2 Corinthians 5:17). No man or woman can come in contact with this powerful God and not change or be challenged to change. It is a blessing to know and to walk with Jesus Christ. I wish I could say that this ended the bitterness with my mom, but I must confess it did not end. The acceptance of Jesus Christ as my Lord and Savior is a wonderful thing that happened to me, but it made life for me more complicated, because now I could no longer blame my father and mother for my actions. I had to now deal with my own fears and doubts. This battle went on for years. I believe God treats us at times, like we might do a banana or an orange. He peels back the hulls to get to the good part of the fruit. God will take us like he found us, but He will not leave you like he found you. He will peel back all that is not like Him to get to that good part of us. A few years after I gave my life to the Lord, my mom got saved also. It was a great thing to have happened for our relationship and our family, but my bitterness and anger had gotten deeper. My mom and I still had problems. Throughout the course of many years, my mom was diagnosed with cancer and later required a caregiver. I took this job unwillingly and begrudegly because I was the oldest. My mom and I fought through three cancer scares. The fourth time, mom said, "Baby, I am tired of fighting." My mom began to apologize to all her children and repent to us one by one. One day, as we were going to Riverdale, Georgia, for a treatment, I asked my mom a question that had puzzled me all my life: "What happened? Why did you treat us the way you did?" And when I heard my mom's story, there was not a dry eye in my car that day. I finally understood something that Solomon said in, "Wisdom is the principal thing; therefore get wisdom; and with all thy getting get understanding" (Proverbs 4:7). I have come to find out that everything becomes easy when you get a good understanding of what you ought to do and what needs to be done. Through this encounter, my mom and I finally developed a relationship that a son and a mother should have. It did not happen overnight, but through time of turmoil and suffering. Please hear me very well. Life is too short and eternity too long for us not to enjoy the freedom that Jesus Christ died for us to have. "Stand fast therefore in the liberty wherewith Christ hath made us free, and be not entangled again with the yoke of bondage" (Galatians 5:1). "There is therefore now no condemnation to them which are in Christ Jesus who walk not after the flesh, but after the spirit" (Romans 8:1). Studying these two scriptures, we can readily see how important it is for us to stay free in our walk with the Lord. The word *steadfast* means "to be unwavering, having a firm grip, firmly fixed." What Paul is saying to us is, "Get a firm grip on your freedom, be unwavering in your freedom." The word *condemnation* means "to express strong approval of, to convict or be pronounced guilty of a crime." Paul is saying to us that if we are in Christ, we are not guilty of the crime anymore. Once we accept Jesus, we are no more convicted of the charges. This is a wonderful place to be in our walk with the Lord.

PERSONAL EXPERIENCES OF OTHERS

In this chapter, I talked to other people about their experiences with bitterness. Everybody has a story to tell. My role as a pastor is to see and counsel people who are drowning in unforgiveness and bitterness. Many people have been stuck there for years, going over the same thing only because they refuse to move on. I hope you enjoy these stories of people who have come through a lot to get to this point to even talk about their hurts. God bless all of you for your insight and your stories.

Joe's Story

My name is Joseph and the root of my bitterness began in my life, when my mother died from sickle cell anemia. As a child, I did not have a real relationship with my mother. I did not know how she looked or the sound of her voice. I only knew my mom from the pictures that my family had of her. There was a lot of emptiness as I became older. It was very easy for me to become bitter since I knew I would never touch, talk, or feel what a mother's love really was. My sister told me that the doctor told my mom not to give birth to me because her life was at risk. She already had six children, but she gave birth to me anyway, I believe that's why she named me Joseph Paul, like in the Bible. It was hard for me not to be bitter since my mom died two years after I was born. But God, in his mercy, still took care of me and made ways for me through it all. My grandmother and grandfather loved me unconditionally. My grandmother gave me love as if she was my real mother. My grandfather taught me how to be a man and how to love God. This helped me a whole lot as a teenager because my dad and I did not have a good relationship like a father and son should have. My dad was mentally and physically abusive to me. Because I lived with my grandfather and grandmother, this caused a separation between my siblings and me. Because of this separation, my bitterness grew deeper and deeper toward my family. But as I have gotten older, the relationship between my siblings and I is better now. I was born with a speech impediment that caused me to have low–self esteem. Having this speech disorder affected me in school and my relationships with people. I was afraid of being made fun of by others. I remember once when I was in elementary school and it was my time to read out loud in the front of all my classmates, mentally, I felt like I was standing in front of a firing squad getting ready to be shot. This was a terrible experience for me to go through. Not one word came out of my mouth; and this caused the other kids to laugh and make fun of me, and that hurt real bad. I dreaded Easter season because I knew my grandmother would get me a speech, and this also was a horrible experience for me to endure. My way of dealing with all this was by becoming angry. My temper was out of control. If anyone pushed me the wrong way, it was on. Another way I dealt with all my pain was to make people laugh, but none of these things helped me. Only when I accepted Jesus Christ as my Lord and Savior did things began to change for me. God gave me some tools to work with. First, he placed me in a great ministry with great leaders. My, pastor having dealt with bitterness in his personal life, began to teach us how to be free from it. Secondly, I learned how to fast and pray, which will destroy the yoke of the enemy. Thirdly, I have a daily reading of God's Word, which is our daily food for our spirit. I just went through another time when bitterness tried to come in again. I was diagnosed with cancer; but with the prayers of my pastor, my First Lady, who is my Pastor's wife, and my wife, God brought me through it. I am now cancer–free, and all glory goes to God.

Sarah's Story

I used to be very bitter toward my dad for never being there, even though he lived with us when I was younger. I was also bitter about the harsh upbringing he took us through, when it seemed like he was not living what he preached. As I got older, I realized how much money was required to take care of a family of six and a young church. Then I became pregnant and realized that some of his warnings were for my good.

After my parents divorced, I was torn between bitterness and guilt. I felt guilty and often times thought about what if I had tried a little harder to keep the laundry clean and dinner ready every night, maybe my dad would have been happy and stayed. At the same time, I was bitter with my mother for making me do what I thought was her job while she watched soap operas all day. Through all this, I turned inward and became self-absorbed with music. I cried so much that one night, I decided my tears were not doing anyone any good and made a vow that I would not cry anymore about anything. I found comfort in gospel music and kept my feelings to myself. Secretly, inside, I was raging with anger and bitterness.

Over the next five years, I continued to internalize all of my feelings and anger and bitterness continued growing in my heart and life. No one would have known this because I was always smiling and laughing outwardly. One day, after receiving a notice of eviction because my mother had upset the landlord, I decided I wanted freedom. I thought I could get it by getting away from my family. What I did not realize was that the problem was inside of me. Someone once said, "He who angers you controls you." I came to find out that there is truth and reason to that saying. I moved out of my mother's house, but my mother did not move out of my head, heart, or spirit.

At this point in my life, my dad had been physically absent for a long time. I did visit him once. After he left, I had a long, hard cry. Crying was something I had not done in a long time. I cried because I found out he was bipolar. I realized everything I had held against him in my heart were issues that may have been beyond his control. This bitterness, hatred, hurt, and pain really had no substance because my dad's mental state made up a lot of who he had been to me over the years. His irrational thinking now made sense to me.

My mother did not want me to move out, partially because I would not be able to collect on the child support that had stopped years before. But I decided that I wanted to move on physically and emotionally. I moved into my own apartment and wrote my dad, letting him know I forgave him for the things I felt he had been wrong. I just wanted to be free in my heart.

I began to realize also that tears serve more purpose than cleansing the eye; they also help cleanse the heart. I realized that my dad's bipolar disorder would not allow him to understand my point, so I let it go. Being free from bitterness toward my dad was very freeing to me emotionally. But I still had years of anger and bitterness toward my mother to deal with. I found it is harder to get over something when it is constantly in your face.

I got married to a man who did not believe in letting anyone control him mentally or emotionally. I thank God for my husband. He refused to allow the struggles and challenges he went through with his first wife to affect or influence our relationship. What he experienced in that marriage enabled him to help me. Ant would tell me to stand up for myself, and it would help me heal. But my bitterness was so deeply rooted that I felt like a five-year-old inside, when I would talk to my mother. He would pump me up, but when I went to face my mother, my fear would paralyze me while I secretly raged inwardly. Around this time, I was really crying out to God to make me free. I talked to a friend, Valeria Stubbs. She told me I needed to take back my vow not to cry because it would help me heal. I wanted to be free so badly that I would do whatever I needed to do. So I prayed, telling God I was sorry for quenching the gift of tears. I know He gave them to me for a reason, and I wanted them to flow again. Suddenly, I began to cry about all kinds of things; it felt good. Years of built-up tears began cleansing me and making me whole in many areas of my life. When I say whole, I'm speaking in terms of maturity. But tears alone did not get it. One day, while reading devotion, I came across this scripture: "Be gentle with one another, sensitive. Forgive one another as quickly and thoroughly as God in Christ forgave you" (Ephesians 4:32, (Message Bible). So I looked up the definition of *forgive*. It read, "To cease to feel resentment against." I realized that I was an active participant in feeling bitter. All this time, I was blaming my parents; but at this moment I realized that I could stop even if they did not stop doing and saying things toward me. I wanted to be free at any cost. Holding all this anger, bitterness, and resentment inside only tormented my mind and, while the offender slept peacefully at tonight. I asked God to help me. I told Him I forgave my mother for everything. Suddenly, a weight lifted. I felt freer than I had ever felt. I e-mailed my mother and told her I forgave her of all the things I felt she had done and said wrong toward me. I told her she did not have to understand why I had felt bitter and angry for years. She just needed to know I was working toward freedom and I forgave her. I also asked her to forgive me for anything I had done or said wrong against her. Hurting people hurt other people. After having children, I decided I wanted to break the generational curse and impart love into my children. I could not do this from a position of hurt and bitterness.

I cannot say that I do not get angry anymore toward my mother, but I can say that I do not harbor it in my heart. Just yesterday, at thirty-one years old, I thought of something that could have brought a new wave of negative emotions. But I consciously decided to let the past stay in the past. When I did not let it affect me, I realize how much I have grown.

Now that the bitterness is gone, there is more room for love in my heart. I can love others more because I allowed God to fill me with love. I try not to continue to rehearse the past because I do not want to be bound by it anymore. Thank God for freedom. My husband and I are happier. I can enjoy the good things God wants for me.

Maria's Story

Bitter is defined as "hard to bear, grievous, distressful, hard to admit or accept, resentful, or cynical" (Dictionary.com). Being bitter is something I can relate to very much. I have dealt with many things in my life, including rejection, family hurts, divorce, eviction, and not being understood. All of these things have caused me, at some point in my life, to be bitter. When dealing with the challenges that arose in my life, I placed a mental wall, block, or barrier in my mind, so I don't remember them. The three people who cause me to remember the bitterness and pain from my past, I keep those people at a distance. Many of the hurts that I have dealt with in my life, I have had to let God deal with them because they were like scars that had healed on the outside but, still oozed with infection, pain, and hurt on the inside. When situations arise that remind me of my past, it makes me shut down and become less receptive. A good example is this year's youth revival. We had a preacher who preached well. However, due to his method of delivering the Word, it reminded me of my father. As a result, I found myself having a difficult time receiving the Word.

Dealing with hurts and bitterness is a continuous thing. Now that I am heading toward marriage, many times, my fiancé and I talk about things like that and how they have caused us to become bitter. I must continually watch myself because my reactions to those around me will be negative, causing me to hurt others due to my actions or the lack of a response.

There is no easy fix for me when it comes to the issue of bitterness. Some things I pray about are not to become bitter or not to show my hurt toward others. Other things I don't know how to deal with and I just have to leave it in the hands of God. When I leave it in His hands, I pray that He will take care of it and take the sting out of it. I can tell many wounds have been healed. I am less bitter about them. But there are still some areas in my life that simply have a scab on them. The pain and effects of those bitter experiences resurface in my life from time to time. I move forward praying daily not to be bitter or to continue the curse of bitterness in my family.

From when I was a young girl, I was always the black sheep of the family. This may have been because I did not take things at face value and I asked many questions. Another reason might be because I am a little bolder in trying things than my siblings. It might be because I am a little more verbally aggressive with my feelings, thoughts, and emotions. This feeling of being the black sheep of the family is one of the essential causes of a strained relationship between my parents and me. My mother would always tell me I would be the first to get pregnant at a young age, mess up my life, and not go anywhere in life. My dad always told us that we weren't going to be teachers or doctors, but that we would be nothing. Seeing that he was a doctor, that statement about us being nothing made no sense to me. Not only was he a doctor, but he was also a pastor.

Being a preacher's kid allows you to see, hear, and know a lot about church that the average person does not know. Having to balance what the preacher says and what the preacher does was a struggle. We went to every denominational church under the sun. We took religion to the maximum. We wore dollies; we ate the "original" Passover meal each year. and even waved palm branches while singing "Hosanna" each year. We stayed at the altar and called Jesus louder and faster until we got it. This meant you were slobbering all over yourself, your nose was running, and you were lightheaded from inhaling quickly. We wore dark clothes, long skirts, and no makeup. All these things occurred during various times of our lives. At the same time, we had all–saints night for Halloween. When we were wrong on assignment books in junior high, our parents ripped them up and threw them in the fireplace. While they were doing this, we were getting rebuked and the devil got cast out of us. Did I mention my father built an altar in our house? The purpose of the altar was so we could pray at any time. All of these things made me very skeptical and unsure about church, Jesus, and anything related to religion. Through my life, I had to learn to have a personal relationship. I had to learn to lean and talk to Him and that the theatrics surrounding church were symptoms of spiritual people, not a relationship with Jesus.

My father also had a "beat now, talk later" policy. This policy was another issue that caused the curse of bitterness to run rampant in our family. It was bad enough that DEFACS knew us by name, but my mom would write notes asking the teacher to allow us to sit on pillows because the bruising and the desk seats were hard. We would get beat with anything, for any reason, without any questions asked. This made me want to rebel even more. I was going to get a beating whether it was my fault or not.

As I got older, my parents grew apart. Soon after they grew apart, they eventually separated and then divorced. After we moved to Georgia, we endured eviction and living in shelters and housing projects. Going through these things made me stronger. I got past all of that. The thing I can't get past is that my mother refused to work. My sister and I worked for the little money our family had. I can only think that if she tried to work, maybe some of the things we went through we would not have had to gone through. On top of that, she pressed charges against my father and got him locked up for not paying child support. I could not understand why she did that because she didn't support us either. Over the process of time, I found out she tried to get land that was promised to us by my father. She would take our checks and then ask, "Do you pay bills here?" With her, it was always, "Do as I say, not as I do."

I have come a long way though the prayers of my Pastor, First Lady, and personal relationships. I am nowhere near where I feel like I could be, but I'm definitely far from where I was. I'm delivered from bitterness, but I must keep my mom at a distance. Just last week, she asked me to come and spend time with her, but I ignored it. I made a promise to myself every day not to become like her. I would love to have a relationship with her.

Nikitta's Story

The ability to forgive is making the choice to give up or exhaust all ill feelings that one might have against someone, total loss of memory regarding the situations, to let go, to release. I was sitting in service one Sunday hearing my pastor preach the Word, when I came to the realization that bitterness had developed in my life. At that time, I really didn't even know what bitterness was. I had to go to Webster's dictionary to get a better understanding of the meaning of bitterness. After pondering the message and the meaning of the word, I knew I had to be delivered and forgive the people, events, and circumstances in my life that had made me bitter. At this particular time, the task of forgiving was not a part of my life. I could say I forgive a person all day long, but the act of forgiving was not in my heart. The inability to forgive could have possibly destroyed my life. Colossians 3:13 states, "Forbearing one another, and forgiving one another, if any man have a quarrel against any; even as Christ forgave you, also do ye." How was I, with my mean old self, going to do this? This one thing had hit me. It hit me so hard that I became hungry and anxious to know more about it so I could be set free. I wanted to get free from things that had me secretly bound and locked up in bondage. Now I was seeking and waiting to become free. Studying the Word more has helped to make this task obtainable. Luke 6:37 says, "Judge not, and ye shall not be judged; condemn not, and ye shall not be condemned: forgive, and ye shall be forgiven." After reading this passage of Scripture, that was enough for me. I wanted God to forgive me for all of my many sins.

I had no clue how I was going to accomplish the task of truly forgiving people. Choosing not to forgive only hurts the person choosing not to forgive, not the other people. Hurting people will hurt other people. Holding on to the past hurts, and disappointments can only destroy a person's destiny. I had to learn that new friendships will never be able to be established due to unforgiveness. Life itself brings along its fair share of hurts. When life brings those hurts, we must be willing to confront and deal with the issue at hand. Having the right attitude, being able to show love, assures that once you release the hurt, God will heal and deliver. Healing begins immediately after choosing to forgive. Learning to implement the power of forgiveness and making it a part of one's daily life is the key to conquering this spirit.

Hurt is not avoidable. It is just a part of life that we must learn to master. We must learn to confront issues that control us and deal with the root of the problem. In my forgiving people for the wrongs they committed towards me, I also had to learn to forgive myself. As I began to recognize the spirit of bitterness and the effects of it, it became apparent that it had begun to affect the relationships in my home. I had become bitter with my own parents and siblings. Being the youngest of three children, I received all the spankings and punishments regardless of the situation. I was always blamed. This thing lingered on throughout my adulthood. I built a block out of the hurts that occurred due to my childhood experiences. I never allowed people to get close to me, and I did not trust anyone. I found myself withdrawing from my family and refusing to show them love. The inability to show love and my need to stay withdrawn made it hard for me to fellowship with my brothers and sisters in the Lord. This seed of bitterness that had taken hold of my life was controlling every area of my life. I met this man that preached a word that pricked my spirit and opened the door that delivered me from the bitterness I was battling with my family. But some time after I resolved that issue of bitterness, another situation arose in my life that brought this issue back to life.

At the age of twenty-four, I found myself living in a dark closet that was filled with anger, disappointment, bitterness, confusion, and several unanswered questions. Having my best friend taken away from me at such a young age and not fully understanding why or how this could happen, I found myself blaming none other than God. At this point, I was not even sure of who God was or if he was even real. For years, I heard people say that God was real and that everything happens because of him. I was angry with him for taking away someone that I loved. Not even knowing the seriousness of being angry with God, I was killing myself without having a physical weapon, reigniting the pain of past hurts. How could I trust God? At that moment, I felt as if I died. I had no reason to live a breathless life. Isolating myself from people and not wanting to talk to anyone were a constant way of life for me. I felt like nothing could ease the pain that I felt. I thought no one could do anything to straighten out this now–twisted mind.

My mind had been held hostage by mental torture for three years. I found myself neglecting my very own child due to this drastic challenge that life had tossed my way. I did not have the power to think clearly. My mind was twisted like a tightrope with no end. Anything I did in life consisted of what I now know is sin. Sin became my name. A life of partying, sex, and using and selling drugs were the things that I did to try to disguise the pain. I felt inside like a battered person screaming for help and looking for love. The outer appearance was that of someone with it all together. Suicidal thoughts danced in my mind. I was raised in the church. There I was at battle in my mind with those thoughts and all I could do was cry out for help like a toddler. All I could think is will someone please help me? I knew the life that I was living was not right. Lord, I know I am hell bound.

God allowed this lady on my job who had always tried to witness to me to cross my path once again. She began to ask me if I knew Jesus. My reply was, "I am upset with God. I have been for quite some time. I really don't know if he is real." At that moment, she began to explain to me who He is and said if I would totally surrender my life to Him and trust Him, I would have eternal life. This conversation opened the door for God to heal the brokenness that was felt for years and to restore the love that I once had for myself.

Finally, I had the courage to attend church with the angel that was sent my way. That day was the best day of my life. Upon entering this church, the ushers were there with smiling faces and warm hugs; and there was an overall the presence of love in the air. I was thinking *this cannot be real. I must be dreaming.* After attending this church for a while, I found this to be the norm. Even the Pastor and First Lady showed so much love to me, a total stranger. Several months had passed. I began to listen to the word that was beating my flesh week after week. Despite the tireless beatings by the Word, it sure did make me feel good to know that I had been living wrong and someone was concerned enough about me to encourage me and tell me that I must and could do better. I knew this was definitely the place where I wanted to be, a place of restoration. Ephesians 1:18 states, "The eyes of your understanding being enlightened; that ye may know what the hope of his calling is, and what the riches of the glory of his inheritance in the saints." There is hope for my life, a life of pure bliss, only if I use the road map that God has designed for every man who chose to read it and apply himself to the rules and regulations. Romans 12:1–2 states:

> I beseech you therefore, brethren, by the mercies of God, that ye present your bodies a living sacrifice, holy, acceptable unto God, which is your reasonable service. And be not conformed to this world: but be ye transformed by the renewing of your mind, that ye may prove what is that good, and acceptable, and perfect, will of God.

I now have a better understanding about dealing with the weight of bitterness. New friends have now come into my life, and I never thought I would reach a place to where I would call someone my friend. I have let my walls slowly fall down in my life when it comes to dealing with people. Ephesians 4:32 says, "And be ye kind one to another, tenderhearted, forgiving one another, even as God for Christ sake hath forgiven you."

Marikah's Story

Many five–year–olds don't have to grow up fast. All they have to do is be cute and have no care in the world. Well, when I was five years old, I had to grow

up very fast. At that time, my mom and dad were getting a divorce. I remember everything about that day, but I guess that's the only thing I remembered about my mother because I didn't know her very well. All I remember is my daddy picking me up in our van to take me to school. Back then I was in pre–k; but because of my height, they moved me up a grade.
So when my daddy carried me in his arms, all I remember him saying is, "Marikah and Jalil, we're going on a little trip."

I guess me and Jalil were thinking the same thing because he asked my dad, "Where is Sharonda?"

Sharonda was my half–sister and was twelve at the time. My dad was silent, so we didn't ask anything else. Like most little kids, we fell asleep; and when I woke up, we were in North Carolina with my Auntie Bonita and Uncle Jerome, whom I had never seen before.

My daddy asked them if they would take care of me and my brother for a little while. My daddy was a Navy Seal but had gotten out after serving eleven years and took a job in Hawaii. Jalil and I stayed in North Carolina for four to six months while my dad was working in Hawaii. He sent money to my auntie and uncle for my brother and me. My daddy, being raised to be a responsible black man, came back to get me and my brother. I thought we were going back home to Jacksonville, Florida; but instead, we moved in with my grandmother in Griffin, Georgia, where my daddy was raised.

From 1998 to 1999, we lived in Griffin, Georgia. Because my daddy was a good man and took care of his own kids, his family didn't mind helping out with us. My daddy's family took us to Sunday school, Sunday service, Bible study, revivals, etc. My daddy's family is still to this day church–going people.

I remember one Mother's Day service I leaned over to a lady sitting beside me and asked her to help me pray that God would send me a mother, not knowing that on July 1, 2000, that same lady would become my stepmother. Isn't that a small world? With the marriage, I gained three more brothers: Charles, Matthew, and Joshua. They took seven days for their honeymoon. My stepbrothers stayed at their auntie's, and my brother and I stayed with our aunties. I thought it was heaven on earth until the honeymoon was over. My dad, Jalil, and I moved to Austell, Georgia, with my stepmother and my new stepbrothers. This is where our new journey began.

I was seven at this time and didn't quite know what the heck was going on. All I saw was our stuff being moved onto a truck headed far from Griffin,

Georgia,. I really was going to miss the simple life we had in Griffin. Now we were living in a new house in an area with people we had to learn to get along with. It was going to be a crazy ride.

The first year of marriage was full of misunderstandings and just plain *hell* on earth, arguments, fights, and lots of crazy feelings that I can't even began to explain. God really had to help us with that first year. Jalil and I had to learn to follow Mama Shun. Charles, Matthew, and Joshua had to learn how to follow my dad. Basically, it was the Morgans vs. Ransoms for a few years. All of us tried to get along with each other, but it was very hard. The one thing that always kept us close was early Saturday morning prayer. Mama Shun started Saturday morning prayer and family forum with her boys when they were little, and she continued with us. She would wake us up early to pray and read the Bible. Afterward, we would do our chores and clean the whole house. It was basically our family time.

When I reached a certain age, I started thinking about my mom. What's her name? What is she like? Why were we not with her? The usual stuff any child would think of. I remember one summer my dad let me and my brother spend a few weeks with her. I guess I was so used to Mama Shon's ways that I was free but, at the same time, uncomfortable. When we got up there, my sister was pregnant and my mom had some lady with her. I was little, so I thought it was just a friend. That was the summer that everything changed. My sister, Sharonda, was still pregnant but was moving to New York to be with her child's father. My mom's "friend" was living with her, so I saw her all the time. The most important part I remember was taking my sister to the bus station. We were still at home, and my sister told me to go inside my mother's room and wake her up. My brother tried to stop me, but my sister said, "No. Marikah has to know." So I went inside my mother's room, and I couldn't believe my eyes. My mom and her friend were laying in the same bed. I grew up in church, and I remember my uncle, Pastor H.L. Morgan, saying only men and women were supposed to be sleeping with each other. So I walked over on her side and tapped her to wake her up. When my mom saw me, she was shocked. When my mom saw me, she told me to hurry out of her room and then go stay with my sister and brother in the living room. As soon as my mom got dressed, we went to the bus station to drop my sister off. Before my sister got on her bus, we said our good-byes; and then she took off. That was the last time in a long time I ever saw her.

That next morning, me and Jalil had to go back home.

When we finally drove up to the airport, my mom let us out with our bags and said, "Ya'll be safe. I love ya'll. I'll miss you a lot."

I, holding my brothers hand, asked, "Aren't you coming with us?"

She said, "No, baby girl. Sorry, but I have to stay with her." She pointed at her friend. "But ya'll be safe now. Now go on inside. I don't want ya'll to miss ya'll's flight."

I was just standing there in shock.

Jalil, still having a hold of my hand, bent down and said, "It'll be okay, Marikah. I won't let anything happen to you."

We turned around and started walking to the airport. That was the last day I ever saw or talked to my mom.

When we came back, I was mad and crying at the same time. I told my dad and Mama Shun everything that happened to us. Then Mama Shun told me something I still don't understand to this day.

"Marikah, your mother is gay. The lady that was sleeping with your mother was her lover."

I was extremely angry. I was that kind of mad that causes you to cry; but for some reason, no tears came out. That was the day I stopped crying all together. I was so mad because I was living with family who always kept stuff away from me. They didn't understand that I wasn't a little girl any more but a girl who had things going for herself who wanted to be told the truth.

I continued to grow up without saying anything to my mother. Also at this time, I was giving Mama Shon hell—disobeying her, talking back; I was doing it all. You can pretty much say I was a bad child at home, doing whatever I felt like doing, fighting all of my brothers, not being a good daughter, not being a good little/big sister. The devil had a good hold on me.

I had rejection problems; I really didn't know what love was. So I started going with this boy. Man, was he fine; light–skinned, hot, and dreamy. I just fell in love. I knew him since I was nine years old. The first time I saw him, I knew I was in love. I know I was young then. That's why it was called puppy love. We went out when we were ten, thirteen, fourteen, and fifteen. My family said I was a fool for going with him. At that time, I really didn't see what they were talking about. He cheated on me. I just forgave him. He would flirt with other girl's right in front of my face; and still, I took him back. He did so much to me that it hurt; but because I was so in love with him, I really didn't care about my health. But instead, I did everything in my power to let him stay with me. I remember the night he told me he loved me. I just ran to my mom (Mama Shon) and told her what I thought was good news. She told me something that I'll never forget.

She said, "Marikah, he don't love you. If he loves you, then he won't mentally and physically hurt you."

I finally understood what she was talking about. When we finally broke up, I never went with him again. I was really heartbroken. That was the first person I ever loved, and he misused it. I learned that I was too young and there are more fish in the sea. Also, I learned that my family and God will always love me no matter what.

Now at this point of my life, my oldest brother, Charles, was doing his thing; Jalil, my second–oldest brother, left me and went to Florida to live with our mother. Matthew, my third–oldest brother, was a senior at Pebblebrook High School; and Joshua, my youngest brother, was an eighth–grader at Sandtown Middle School with Mama Shun, who worked there. I was in the second semester of ninth grade at Pebblebrook High School. I was still hurt because my ex–boyfriend was not mine anymore, Jalil left me and never checked on me, I had no friends and don't know anybody at that school, and I didn't have my best friends with me anymore. I was just like a lost puppy with nowhere to go. By the end of semester, I was trying out for JADE; and after tryouts, I went to church. I think my uncle, Pastor H.L. Morgan, was preaching that night. After the service, I wanted to change my ways.

I was tired of being alone. I had to put God back in my life. All the trouble I went through and all that pain, I just gave up. I reunited with God, and my life was getting better.

After a year went by still not talking to my mom, the devil was throwing stuff at me. Smoking, sex, drinking, and every other tactic the devil threw at me I fell prey to it. I remember a one point I failed God and started using pills to kill myself. I was at a very dark place in my life. But I stopped when I heard my favorite gospel song, "I Trust You." I fell on my knees and cried my heart out to God, saying sorry. From then on, I kept my faith. Sometimes the devil tried to do it again; but I always said, "I trust my God. All I'm going through is in vain. I will never give up."

Now that I am sixteen years old and in the tenth grade, I have no worries anymore. When I look back through my life, I see everything that was done. It was because I was still mad, hurt, confused, and bitter toward my mother. I haven't seen her since I was eleven years old. She never called to ask if I was okay, to talk to me about stuff, to just say hello, nothing. Sometimes I feel like I am the child she never wanted. It feels like the only people she really cares about and talks to are Sharonda and Jalil. But I have no worries because God gave me a stepmom in my life who is a godly woman, and I surely thank Him for that. She might be tough, but the reason is because she wanted all her children to be great. I didn't realize that until now. Right now, I want to thank her so much for not giving up on me. Mama Shun and my auntie, First Lady Morgan, truly showed me what a Proverbs 31 woman is. Thank you.

On March 18– 21, 2010, bitterness in my heart for my mother was gone. During those days was our youth revival. There was a powerful pastor named Elder Robert Taylor who preached at our youth revival. He made me want to live totally for God and to finally forgive my mom. I had bitterness for my mom my whole life. I even hurt the people I love because of that. But thanks to God he changed everything about me. I'm still working on some other things that I'm bitter about, but at least I finally throw away the one that really hurt me.

Serenity's Story

Some people say that children around seven or eight years old never go through anything. Well, guess what? They are so wrong. When I was born, my mom and dad were not married. So I am a child born out of wedlock, which brought on other challenges for me to understand. I was born in Spalding Regional Hospital. Any young child would like to look to see pictures of your father being there to cut the umbilical cord and signing your birth certificate; but my dad was at Clemson University, playing football. Later, he went on to play in the Canadian football league for eight or nine years. During this time, I very rarely saw my father. I do remember my grandma taking me to my father's games at Clemson. She would dress me up like the Clemson cheerleaders. I was around three or four years of age. I remember jumping up and down, screaming, "Run, Daddy, Run." But for some reason, my father just stopped coming to see me. This was another struggle I had to deal with at a young age. I used to look at other kids with their dads, laughing and playing. I wanted that, and that was something I couldn't have at the time. I missed my daddy so much. The lack of a relationship with my father and my desire to have a relationship with him soon made me start disliking my father very slowly. I had gotten to the point where I didn't even want to talk to him or see him.

One Sunday, I was at church and my granddad started preaching a message on bitterness. I just broke down crying because bitterness was trying to take over my life. I knew that having bitterness in my heart was wrong. My granddad called for an altar call. I went down there with tears.

He said to me, "You are real bitter with someone."

I broke down more. He prayed for me. He told me it was time for me to forgive. I went to my dad and gave him a hug. It felt like a ton of weight was lifted off my shoulders.

Now my dad and I are the best of friends. I can tell him anything. I can call him for anything now. When I am feeling down, I know I can call my dad. He will be there for me and say, "It's going to be okay, princess." There have been times I have felt like the whole world was on my shoulders.

When I was a child, I was overweight. I was considered fat, for my age. People used to tease me all the time for this. Well, this also added to the bitterness that I was already carrying. People gave me nicknames like fatty, big bird, big girl, etc. It had begun to get overbearing. One day, I got home and saw some pills on my dresser. I was about eleven years old at this time. The devil kept telling me to take the pills. He said to me, "No one cares for you, and nobody loves you." So as I was about to take the pills, I heard someone say, "Don't lose hope; this is not the way." I didn't do it. But after that, I went through a very heavy depression at the age of thirteen years old. By the time I was going to swallow a handful of pills, my little sister came in my room. I didn't take them when I saw her. She gave me a reason to live. I knew if I had done this, my sister, Miyah, would have suffered more than anyone not having her oldest sister with her. By this time, I had gained a little confidence but not as much as I should have. The reason I was depressed was because I felt that I was fighting a battle all by myself. I was losing friends that I loved dearly and cared so much about. It was getting harder and harder for me to bare. My friends that I had known since we were babies in diapers were no longer people that I could call friends.

One day at church, my grandpa preached on letting go. At that moment, I realized that sometimes I have to let go of those people who were in my life to bring me down. So at that point, I had gotten over my depression; but it seemed as though the devil always put obstacles in my way.

Another time I had to deal with bitterness was with my mom when she had gotten married. This wonderful and new marriage was great to her, but it brought me a stepdad. Well, my stepdad and I didn't get along very well. We always argued, fussed, and had major attitudes whenever we were in the same house at the same time. I didn't like the fact of him taking my place with my mom. He was also taking the place of being my dad in a certain kind of way. I did not want him to discipline me. I did not feel like he had the right to because he was not my father. I didn't even want him to talk to me, to be honest about it. It had gotten so bad we could go days and not say a word to each other. One day I was talking to my grandma about the situation. She told me I had to start doing what he told me even though I didn't want to. She said even though it might not seem right to me, I had to do what he said because I was a child. I had to learn to stay in a child's place. She said it might be hard but I had to keep praying and the Lord would pull me through it. So I prayed as much as I could. My prayers were answered. My stepdad and I are close now. We don't argue or fuss like we used to. I think this happened because we have gotten to know each other better.

The devil did not stop there. My mom and I had a great relationship once upon a time; but for some reason, all of that changed. I started feeling as though my mom didn't like me. I felt she was never there for me. It seemed to me that she would not listen to me when I had a problem. It seemed to me that she was there for other people; but when it came to me, she wasn't there. It shocked me and hurt me that my mom would act like that. You would think she was listening to me when I had a problem. I would even think that she would allow me to lie on her shoulders and cry. I would expect a dad to not listen or not to care. But in my case, it was totally different. I've always tried to talk to my mom. But many times, I would stop because it would always end up in an argument. So I found myself talking to everybody else but her. I hated that because, if anybody, I should be able to talk to her. I prayed again, and God came through for me. My mom and I talked and got everything situated. Our relationship is healing one day at a time. I believe that my mom and I will have a good relationship again because the grace of God is over our lives. Some people don't fully understand why young people have to go through so much. This is the reason why the suicide rates are high now among teens. The typical adult doesn't ask his or her child what struggles they are going through. I have had close friends die because they felt no one would understand or listen to them. The Bible says in St. John 10:10, 'The devil comes to steal, kill, and destroy,' Jesus said, 'but I have come that you may have life and have it more abundantly.'" He tried to steal my destiny, kill me and my soul, and destroy my life; but God was on my side the entire time. I am learning that God will never leave me or forsake me. I overcame my struggles to help people understand that God wouldn't put more on us than we can bear. Through all the good and the bad times, God has been there for me every step of the way. All my struggles have given me wisdom to deal with things with my head held high. I guess you can say that God and my struggles have brought out the best in me.

Lachion's Story

I was trapped in a web of bitterness for several years. I worked with a large corporation for fifteen years. Over the course of this period, I worked in several different departments. While working in the community affairs department, I can recall being caught in a web of bitterness. It took the Word of God to comfort me and guide me to victory. The community affairs department only consisted of four ladies who coordinated volunteer projects for the corporation. My job as office manager was to ensure that over five thousand corporate contributions were processed into the computer system, maintain a large filing system, and assist the department director with meetings and travel arrangements. God gave me favor with the department director. I worked as her administrative assistant in the internal audit department prior to her promotion to community affairs. I was asked to go with her to her new assignment. She would promote me to office manager. I entered this department with excitement and readiness to take on new challenges; however, I was met with strong resistance and opposition from the two ladies who were already there. They were unwilling to accept me and failed to communicate with me unless it was absolutely necessary. During staff meetings, they would openly attack my project ideas and solutions to problems in the office. Many times, I would witness them laughing and talking together; and when they saw me coming toward them, all of sudden, they would get quiet. Of course, this behavior lead to feelings of rejection, which slowly turned into a root of bitterness. The spirit of bitterness wore my spirit down, and it became a heavy burden to go to work and be a productive member of the team. I found myself dreading going to work on a job I once loved. I became very angry and felt powerless to change the situation. One morning, while praying about this problem on the way to work, God reminded me of His Word. He said in Romans 12:21, "Be overcome of evil, but overcome evil with good." When I got the chance, I re–read the whole chapter. God again showed me something in this chapter. Romans 12:19: "Dearly beloved avenge not yourselves, but rather give place unto wrath for it is written, Vengeance is mine, *I will repay*,' said the Lord." The Lord revealed to me that I should not allow their evildoings to paralyze me and keep me from doing good. God charged me to love my enemy and do good to those who despitefully use me. I allowed bitterness, anger, and rejection to paralyze me. Those emotions hindered me from doing good because these spirits were entering into my heart. I found myself trapped in a web of bitterness, convinced in my heart that there was nothing I could do to change the situation. This made me even more depressed. I could not let the light of Jesus Christ shine in darkness and make a difference in a paralyzed state of heart and mind. Matthew 5:16 says, "Let your light so shine before men that they may see your good works and glorify the father which is in heaven." God directed me to purchase a beautiful poinsettia arrangement for Joan, who had a birthday that same week. In obedience, I purchased it along with a cheerful birthday card and placed it on her office desk the evening before. When she arrived to work the next day, she was quite surprised. Her response to my token of obedience as;

Who remembered my birthday? It certainly could not be the one that I have rejected all this time.

There was no way that I could have done this without the help of God's Word. Shortly after this, Joan apologized for the way she had treated me because she had allowed the other lady, Vickie, to convince her to ignore and to reject me; but God's Word is true. When I saw this great breakthrough, I became free to shine the light of Jesus Christ again. Joan and I worked together on many projects and became good friends. We always talked about our children and our hopes and dreams for them. One thing she had that I didn't have was grandchildren. She loved them so much. When she was diagnosed with breast cancer, she felt free enough to share this private moment with me. The director of the department, Becky, received another promotion to vice president of compensation and benefits. a unit of HR. Again, she asked me to go with her. I was made executive assistant to the V.P. of Compensation and Benefits. However, shortly after the promotion, she left. Joan was determined to be a blessing to me. She recommended me for a prestigious chairman's award for the work I had done in community affairs. She had the chance to present to me the prize that I won, which was a large monetary gift. She also gave my boys many gifts. Just look how God turned evil into good only because I dared to trust God and his Word. Joan and I remained close friends until her death from cancer. What a mighty God we serve. His Word is a light unto our feet and a guide unto our pathway. God said in Isaiah 55:8, "'For my thoughts are not your thoughts, neither are your ways my ways,' saith the Lord." It seemed unfair and foolish to me to buy something for someone who was rejecting me. But I did not realize that it was God's way of tearing down the hedge of hatred and bitterness I had built around my heart.

It is amazing to me that the spirit of rejection can leave and revisit our lives from time to time according to the different people we deal with and the circumstances we face. It seems the closer the person might be, the deeper the wound of bitterness and unforgiveness goes. Regardless, we must stay focus on the Lord, Jesus Christ. Proverbs 18:10 says, "The name of the

Lord is a strong tower and the righteous run unto it and are safe." So I give all the glory to God for showing me the power of obedience to His Word and for giving me the mind to obey and experience His victory. The same faithful God has done these things for me before, and He will continue to do them again and again.

Chamise Sweeting
How I Dealt with Bitterness

Bitterness is something I know all too well. I have had several incidences throughout my life that have caused me to have bitterness or show bitterness.

When I was eight years old, I found out that my mom was using drugs. Back then, it wasn't advertised as much as it is today. I noticed that she would act different at certain times of the day. She would not be coherent. She wouldn't be able to hold a conversation or even pay attention. She would also pace back and forth and check all of the doors and windows. As I watched her, I noticed that she hid all of her drugs and smoking tube devices. I would find cans with holes in the middle, small bags with powder residue inside, and her thumbs would be burnt and black like coal. I would take what I found and smash it, break it up, and leave it on the dresser. I wanted her to know that I had found it. I wanted her to realize she wasn't hiding anything from us.

Seeing my mom like this really scared me. The behavior she displayed made me a very nervous child. Sometimes when I would be on my way home from school, I used to wonder, *Okay. Will Mom be at home? Will I have to cook? Will she be high? Which man would be there today?* After a couple of years of living like this, I vowed to myself that I would never be the type of mom that I had. I made a promise to myself never to treat my kids that way.

When I was in fifth or sixth grade, I had a babysitting job. I remember taking my money that I made to buy groceries for my sister, brothers, and myself. Of course, it wasn't much; but it bought the things we needed to eat. I had to walk to the grocery store to buy dish detergent, Ramen noodles, hamburger meat, and french fries. My mom never held down a steady job. She never had any money. We were always on welfare. We never had hot water or a telephone longer than thirty days. We always had to run to someone else house to use their phone or their mop or borrow some sugar. I can remember once when she had one of her male friends over; he would bring us a bag of groceries. Next, she would repay him by going into the room and closing the door. This particular time, I was taking a bath. I had just poured a pot of hot water in the bathtub and ran a little cold water to make it even, and sat down in the water. Next thing I know, the bathroom door flew open and it was him. My mom's male friend saying, "Che–Che, give me back my five dollars that I gave to you." I said, "If you don't get out of here, I will kill you." My voice got deep. I looked at him dead in his eyes. I think I turned evil or something because I scared myself. He shut the door and left. When I got out, I found that he was gone. I went and told my mom. She said, "I know that he is sorry. He didn't mean it." I just stared at her. I could not believe what she said. She just didn't do anything at all. This let me know that she would have let anything go on. I was not even safe in my own home. I wonder if she even remembers that day. This left me not trusting anyone. I had very low expectations and nothing or no one to look up to.

My grandmother was in town from St. Peter. She knew that I didn't have much of a childhood. She always had to take care of my sisters and brothers. She offered to take me back home with her. I was excited and worried about my sister and brothers too. On the day she was heading back, she told me to pack my bags. She would come and get me. My mom saw me packing and tried to talk me out of it. We argued back and forth at this time. I had lost mostly all of my respect for her. She knew she couldn't tell me anything, least of all stay. So she called over one of my uncles to talk to me. I remember standing there with my luggage in my hand and crying while my uncle said, "Don't leave, Che–Che. Who's going to watch your sister and brothers?" I was getting ready to walk because grandma was taking too long. "You can't leave. We need you to help watch out for your mom. What are they going to do without you? Don't leave right now. Wait a while. Why don't you go in about a year or two?" I looked up to my uncle at that time and trusted in what he said, not realizing if I left that meant that he would have to come and check on my sisters and brothers; so I stayed. I did not want to, but who else was going to do it? Nobody was going to help us. Everybody knew, but nobody was willing to help.

I would go by family houses and overhear them talking about my mom and I, but they didn't have any advice or help. Only, "Poor Che–Che," is what my other family members had to say. Even my school friends knew about my home situation. They would say things like, "I seen your mama walking in the middle of the night. You better tell her to be careful.

I seen your mama hanging out with such and such lady. You know that lady she is on drugs. You might want to tell your mama not to hang out with her." It had gotten so bad that when I was in third grade, my mom and I wore the same size clothes because she had lost so much weight. Shortly after that, she went into rehab. Every time she got out, she would say, "Oh, I will never do that again. That was just a bad time. It will get better. You'll see." Six weeks later, she will be back on it. All of this has made me very bitter and, at the time, very embarrassed and caused low self–esteem.

I know that everybody has two parents and just maybe I could have asked my dad for help or to please come get me. But every time he promised to come, he never did. When I turned about fourteen years old, it finally hit me. My mom was on drugs, but at least she hadn't left us and was still there, facing life; but as for my dad, he was never coming. I truly feel for the young ladies who desire to be with their dads or even just to spend some time with them. I remember that pain. My dad and I, we only speak on birthdays and holidays. I can truly say we are a lot alike. He doesn't have much to say, and I don't have much to say either.

Since my childhood wasn't the best, I noticed some things about myself that I am not proud of. I do not trust anyone nor do I believe in what they say. I wait to see it first. I do not accept money from anybody. I never want it to be said, "You are just like your mama." I don't share my feelings; I just keep everything to myself. I am a loner. I have learned not to carry my feelings on my shoulder and not to get close to anyone.

I started hanging out and going out to the clubs when I was fourteen years old. By the time I was eighteen, I was tired, tired of seeing the same people, tired of going to the same clubs, and tired of doing the same thing from week to week. There was nothing new and no expectations on life.

Where was the hope? Who was coming to teach me how to live and how to carry myself? How much longer would I have to go through that? Maybe that was how life was supposed to be. That is what I wondered within myself for a long time, until one day I was invited by my aunt to come to church. This church was different. The man who preached had authority and did not take sides. This man preached the Word, broke it down, and made it so simple you looked at yourself. He still teaches to this day that you are responsible for your own actions and you are to forgive. If you forgive, the Lord will forgive you.

Once you forgive, it will set you free. You will no longer be bound to your past hurts. When I heard that, it was like weight lifted off of my shoulders. My chest was no longer tight, and I could breathe a little better. And I have been breathing and enjoying life ever since. I am no longer mad at my mom for what she put me through. I truly understand the Lord has a way of making you into what you are to become. I realize now that I did not go through all of that just for me. It is to help and to relate and encourage someone else. I thank you, Apostle H.L. Morgan, and my sweet Co–Pastor, Verlene Morgan, for loving and praying for me and my family. You both have truly made a difference in my life as well as my family's life.

Vickie's Story

Bitterness is commonly associated with a strong feeling of resentment. Webster's dictionary defines bitterness as "experiencing severe pain, grief, regret; exhibiting intense animosity." A very common illness that we all experience at some point in our lives is bitterness. Bitterness can be a result of years of abuse, dysfunctional family relationship, or even the death of a loved one. Oftentimes, we are faced with disappointments in which we have to sort through a tangled knot of emotions. Emotions such as anger, grief, rebellion, or regret that runs through our lives. It is easier to put a smile on our faces and pretend that everything is all right when inwardly; we are bound and tied down with an overwhelming feeling of despair. We feel we were let down and even betrayed by God, wondering how and why He would let us go through such grief. With all these emotions entangling our minds, we find it hard to cope and deal with life. Most of the time, we don't even realize that we are bitter because we have mastered the art of masking the pain and hurt of how we really feel. Bitterness, if not dealt with in the beginning stage, can lead to depression, violence, and even suicidal tendencies. You not only hold grudges against those around you, but you often tend to neglect the care of yourself. Many days you might experience downcast spirits, a heavy heart, and responsibilities that feel overwhelming.

As a child, I experienced situations that caused me to become very bitter and angry with God. At the age of seven, I was in a house fire that left me with scars both inwardly and outwardly. I was trapped in the house in a bedroom; and if it had not been for my stepdad running back into the house to get me, I would not have survived. I remember that as he jumped off the back porch with me, the whole house fell in. I can remember lying in the hospital in so much pain, praying that God would just let me die. It was not God's plan for me to die. Instead, I remained in the hospital for about one month, going through intense rehabilitation. I had second and third–degree burns on over seventy percent of my body, including my face, arms, and legs. About two months after being released to go home, my stepdad began to both physically and sexually abuse me. My mom was working two jobs, and I was left alone with him often. He told me that I owed him for saving my life. I would beg and cry for him to stop, but that only made things worse. He would physically abuse me and my sibling and then threaten to kill us if we told anyone what was going on at home. When I finally told my mom what had been going on, she didn't believe me. Even though she witnessed the physical abuse, it didn't make a difference. She was supposed to protect us; but instead, she left us open to be hurt. She began to make excuses for him; and often, we were told to just do what he said so that we wouldn't be punished. She was also being abused by him and felt like she had to stay in the relationship for stability. As time went by, I became very angry with God. I blamed him for allowing this to happen to me. I found myself praying and asking God, *Why didn't you just let me die? Why are you allowing all this hurt? What did I do to deserve this?* I couldn't understand how this loving God could allow this abuse.

As time went on, I began to repress all the feelings that were running on a rampage within me. I wrapped myself in academics at school because that was my way of blocking out what was going on at home. I despised my mother because I felt like she loved him more than she loved us, her children. I learned coping behaviors to help me be able to function of my own. The abuse continued for several years until my mother finally decided she could not take it anymore.

After leaving him, she went on as if nothing had happened; so I guess she learned to repress it all as well. I built up walls at an early age. I felt like I had to protect my heart from being broken anymore. I was determined that no one else would hurt me that much again. During middle school, I found it hard to develop relationships since I became a loner. Most of my time was spent in a corner with a book. I learned to pretend that everything was all right. I learned to pretend because I was so ashamed to tell anyone what was going on. I didn't want to be laughed at or rejected. I was afraid that people would blame me for it because I failed to tell anyone what was going on. I felt like damaged and unwanted property. My self–

worth was on zero. I believed that nobody loved me, and all I wanted was to die.

By the time I reached high school, my self-esteem had been completely depleted. I began to develop relationships in which I allowed myself to be abused. I felt like it was okay to be physically and emotionally abused. I had learned to repress that type of abuse; so in my mind, it was okay. I was alive physically, but my spirit had been beaten and battered to the point in which I was spiritually dead. I was so hurt and traumatized that I had become numb and brittle. I had no knowledge of what it was like to experience genuine love, compassion, care, or concern. Since I had not experienced real love, I continued to live a life that was broken, battered, anger filled, and very resentful. I was a walking time bomb ready to explode at any moment.

By the time that I turned eighteen years old, I was suicidal. I made several attempts to end my life. One incident that occurred I was living with a friend, still fighting through hurts with my son's father. She lived by a busy highway, and I decided that I was going to walk into traffic and get hit by a car and die. I closed my eyes and began to walk into traffic. I couldn't hear anything. It was like everything was blocked out of my mind. When I opened my eyes, I was in the parking lot of the convenience store on the other side of the highway. All I could do was cry. I was thinking *I can't even do that right.* It was then that I heard God saying, "It's not time for you to die. This is not the plan that I have for your life. You have a purpose for being here." God began to tell me that there was a reason that I had gone through so much in my life. I would be a testimony for others. I didn't understand what purpose was and why I had to encounter so much hurt for it. I prayed to God to seek understanding for His purpose for my life. It was at that point in my life that I began to attend Tabernacle of Joy Miracle Deliverance Center. When I got there, the man of God of that house began to speak life into my life. At first, I thought the church was a nesting ground for more hurt; but instead, it became a place where I encountered genuine love. I found it hard to believe that people could care so much for me and not have hidden motives. I was in ministry for years, listening to the Word of God; but I still couldn't gather the strength or courage to fully open up my heart and allow God to heal and deliver me. I was just a member in church attending, but I would not allow anyone into my life or my heart. I slowly began to realize that as long as I kept my emotions bottled up, there was no chance for true deliverance. The emotional walls that I had built up for so long were beginning to be chipped away by the Word of God.

In the medical profession, we use a term called sclerosing to describe the hardening of plaque around the heart. When there is build up of plaque, it begins to harden; and vessels that carry blood to the heart become blocked, and it diminishes the blood flow. The heart is the most vital organ that influences and sustains life to an individual. My heart had become so closed by bitterness that it diminished the capacity of my heart. My quality of life was almost gone, and my spiritual life was on life support. God had to come in and do a complete spiritual heart transplant. There was so much debris left from the unhealed wounds of abuse, anger, and despair that my heart needed to be removed and a new heart installed.

Forgiveness was the first step toward my healing. I had to learn to forgive; so that I could move out of my past and move into my destiny. I had to forgive not only the people who hurt me, but I had to learn to forgive myself. As time has gone by, through the grace of God, I forgave them and let it all go. I can't say that I have forgotten all of the grief, but I have learned to cope and manage my life. Gathering the courage to be honest, to stop running, to stop hiding, and quit pretending brought about a tremendous freedom. I came empty handed to the Lord, carrying nothing but an open heart. God took my honesty and transformed it into saving grace. Some things in life can be patched up, repaired, or redone; but there are some wounds that are too grievous, some blows that are too shattering, and some rifts that are too wide to be pulled back together. Some hurts leave us permanently wounded and our psyches disfigured, but God's strategy for brokenness is not always repair; instead, growth makes the difference. He grants us the gift of starting over. Some damages that occur in our life cannot be fixed, but things that have died due to the damage can be reborn.

My deliverance was a gift of peace. It came through loving gestures from friends. It came through laughter and tears. Most of all, it came from much prayer and fasting. I found healing through love and forgiveness. As I drew closer to God, He drew closer to me. His spirit dwells in me and I in him; so when I recognize the spirit of bitterness trying to enter in again, I am finally equipped to deal with it. I am no longer a victim of bitterness, but I am an advocate for the healing power of forgiveness. I made amends with the people who hurt me, as well as those I hurt with my bitterness. Each new step of spiritual growth requires us to return to the fundamentals of a spiritual life. We must remember that we are powerless, but God is powerful. My sorrow led to brokenness, which brought humility before God. The brokenness led me to surrender my will and life to Him totally. I let go and let God have his way in my life. God not only restored me, but he recycled my failures and hurts, using them for his purpose.

TWELVE SUGGESTIONS TO CONQUER BITTERNESS

The purpose of this chapter is to give you twelve suggestions designed to help you conquer this spirit. We have seen in the previous chapters how dangerous and detrimental this spirit is to you, as a child of God. Mastering the spirit of bitterness will not be easy for you, but you must devise a starting point to initiate a plan of attack. The spirit of bitterness has tied up your life for many years. It has kept you bound in a cycle of generational curses and feuds. It is time to break this cycle and enter into a phases of spiritual, physical, and emotional freedom.

The first step to conquering bitterness is admitting that you are a bitter person. This admission has to be to God and to yourself. In order for us to get help from God or man, we must first admit, "I am bitter about what happened." Pride keeps us from admitting we are bitter or hurt over what happened. God cannot deal with anything that we are not willing to confront. The admission of hurt or bitterness is not a sign of weakness but a sign of strength.

The second step to conquering bitterness is praying for the people who offended you or caused you to become bitter. Matthew 5:44: "But I say unto you love your enemies, bless them that curse you, do good to them that hate you, and pray for them which despitefully use you, and persecute you." This is a secret I am still learning. When offence comes, the initial response is to become bitter, angry, and vindictive. As children of God, we must fight that human instinct to strike back. Instead of striking back, we must enter into prayer and seek God to bring that spirit of hurt and offence out of our inner man. While praying for those who have caused bitterness to enter into our life, we must pray that God delivers and heals us from the inside out instead of a surface level healing. A surface level healing will cause us to react negatively when we encounter that same incident again, but a deep inner healing will not let us bring old baggage into a new situation.

The third step to conquering the spirit of bitterness is to stop rehearsing the incident. Philippians 3:13: "Brethren I count not myself to have apprehended; but this one thing I do, forgetting those things which are behind, and reaching forth unto those things which are before." The mind is created to remember; so quite naturally, when bad things happen, we replay them. As Christians, we might remember the incident, but we should not give that incident any power. The danger of rehearsing an offence over and over again is trying to figure out what we could have done to change the outcome. We are not God, so it is impossible for us to go back in to time and change the series of events that created the hurt.

The fourth step would be not to seek revenge. Romans 12:19–21:

> Dearly beloved, revenge not yourselves, but rather give place unto wrath; for it is written, "Vengeance is mine; I will repay," saith the Lord. Therefore if thine enemy hunger, feed him; if he thirst, give him drink; for in doing so thou shalt heap coals of fire on his head. Be not overcome of evil, but overcome evil with good.

It is a difficult task not to repay evil for evil. The Bible also instructs us to turn the other cheek. When we are encountering painful and hurtful situation, it's hard not to seek revenge. As Christians, we must remember we reap what we sow. So with this in mind, we have to fight the desire to handle our own battles and allow God to handle those painful situations.

The fifth step is to forgive, knowing that Jesus Christ has forgiven you. St. Mark 11:25: "And when ye stand praying, forgive, if ye have ought against any; that your father also which is in heaven may forgive you your trespasses." The ability to forgive is a necessary attribute for all Christians to have working in their lives. We must recognize that forgiving someone doesn't mean that you forget what he/she has done to you, but it's the ability to not allow what that person has done to you to affect your life.

The sixth step is do not rejoice when something negative happens to your abuser. Proverbs 24:17–18: "Rejoice not when thine enemy falleth, and let not thine heart be glad when he stumbleth: Lest the Lord see it, and it displease him, and he turn away his wrath from him." When an abuser begins to experience problems, tests, trials, or hardships in life, do not think God is avenging you and bring pain to that person's life. The Bible lets us know that God rains on the just as well as the unjust. The godly thing to do is to pray for the abuser, so that things may go well with you.

The seventh step is facing the truth that we have not done all things right. First John 2:8: "If we say that we have no sin, we deceive ourselves, and the truth is not in us." Romans 3:23: "For all have sinned and come short of the glory of God." We are not perfect beings and do not make the right decisions or choices all the time. We hurt people intentionally and unintentionally, so it's impossible to believe that we have not caused pain to another person in life. It's important to recognize that we have sinned and need to repent to God as well as man. The eighth step is to seek God for an understanding of how what happened was meant to be used as an instrument to mold you into what He needs you to be and get you where He needs you to go. Romans 8:28: "And we know that all things work together for good to them that love God, to them who are called according to his purpose." When bad things happen in life, we often ask, "Why?" instead of asking "Who has the happened to me for?" As believers, we know that the steps of a good man are ordered by God. When we enter into a trying situation, we must realize when we come out of it, we will have a testimony. That testimony will be used to bring others out. When God brings us to a hard place in life, He is going to bring us through it.

The ninth step to conquering bitterness is to show the love of God to your offender. St. Matthew 5:43–44: "Ye have heard that it hath been said, 'thou shalt love thy neighbor, and hate thine enemy.' But I say unto you, love your enemies, bless them that curse you, do good to them that hate you, and pray for them which despitefully use you and persecute you." God wants us to kill our enemies, accusers, abusers, and foes with kindness. The love of God will leave the offender confused and will hinder bitterness from taking root in your heart, mind, and spirit. We cannot allow the love of God to wax cold simply because we have thorns in our life that cause us grief.

The tenth step to conquering bitterness is to take heed to what comes out of your mouth. Proverbs 18:21: "Death and life are in the power of the tongue: and they that love it will eat the fruit of it." Acting or reacting in a bitter state will cause people to speak from a place of anger. As Christians, we must realize our words carry power. We can damage people and relationships by the things we allow to come out of our mouths. Once things are spoken into the atmosphere, it is impossible to take them back. When dealing with an issue of bitterness, it is necessary that we ask God to word our mouth. We need God to word our mouth, so that we will not kill the things he is trying to establish in our life.

The eleventh step to conquering bitterness is to start showing forgiveness towards others. Ephesians 4:32: "And be kind one to another, tenderhearted, forgiving one another, even as God for Christ sake hath forgiven you." Colossians 3:13: "Forbearing one another, and forgiving one another, if man have a quarrel against any: even as Christ forgave you, so do ye also." The Bible commands us to forgive if we want to be forgiven. True forgiveness is not saying, "I have forgiven you for what you have done, but I have not forgotten. However, true forgiveness is when I treat you the way you want to be treated and do not hold any ill feelings toward you.

The twelfth step to conquering bitterness is to move on and enjoy life. St. John 10:10: "The thief cometh not but for to steal, kill and destroy, *but I have come that ye may have life and that life more abundantly.*" Romans 8:1: "There is therefore now no condemnation to them which are in Christ Jesus who walk not after the flesh, but after the Spirit." Living an abundant life is impossible when bitterness is ruling our spirit. True and freeing enjoyment comes when we are displaying the love of God to those who have despitefully used us and not just to those people who are our friends and constantly show us love.

SCRIPTURES ON BITTERNESS

In this chapter, I will suggest a few scriptures to read on bitterness maybe in your time of leisure or in your time of studying the Word of God, which is our everyday food.

> Keep thy heart with all diligence; for out of it are the issues of life. Put away from thee a forward mouth, and perverse lips put far from thee
> Proverbs 4:23–24

> The heart knoweth his own bitterness; and a stranger doth not intermeddle with his joy
> Proverbs 14:10

A foolish son is a grief to his father, and a bitterness to her that bare him

                                Proverbs 17:25

Who whet their tongue like a sword, and bend their bows to shoot their arrows, even bitter words

                                Psalm 64:3

If I regard iniquity in my heart the Lord will not hear me. But verily God hath heard me; he hath attended to the voice of my prayer

                                Psalm 66:18–19

Therefore I will not refrain my mouth; I will speak in the anguish of my spirit; I will complain in the bitterness of my soul

                                Job 7c:11

Wherefore is light given to him that is in misery, and life unto the bitter soul

                                Job 3:20

My soul is weary of my life; I will leave my complaint upon myself; I will speak in the bitterness of my soul

                                Job 10:1

Even today is my complaint bitter; my stroke is heavier than my groaning

                                                Job 23:2

And another dieth in the bitterness of his soul, and never eateth with pleasure

                                                Job 21:25

"And she said unto them, 'Call me not Ruth [PLEASANT] call me Mara [BITTER] for the almighty hath dealt bitterly with me'"

                                                Ruth 1:20

And she was in bitterness of soul, and prayed unto the Lord and wept sore

                                              1 Samuel 1:10

Therefore if thou bring thy gift to the altar, and there rememberest that thy brother hath ought against thee. Leave there thy gift before the altar, and go thy way; first be reconciled to thy brother, and then come and offer thy gift

                                          Matthew 5–23–24

Therefore I say unto you, 'What things so ever you desire, when ye pray, believe that ye receive them, and ye shall have them. And when ye

stand praying forgive, If ye have ought against any; that your Father also which is in heaven may forgive you your trespasses. But if you do not forgive, neither will your Father which is in heaven forgive your trespasses'
St. Mark 11:24–26

Husbands love your wives and be not bitter against them
Colossians 3:19

Be ye angry, and sin not: let not the sun go down upon your wrath. Neither give place to the devil. Let no corrupt communication proceed out of your mouth, but that which is good to the use of edifying, that it may minister grace unto the hearers. And grieve not the holy Spirit, whereby ye are sealed unto the day of redemption. Let all bitterness, and wrath, and anger, and clamour and evil speaking, be put away from you, with all malice. And be ye kind one to another, tenderhearted, forgiving one another, even as God for Christ sake hath forgiven you.
Ephesians 4:26–29, 32

Follow peace with all men, and holiness, without which no man shall the Lord; Looking diligently lest any fail of the grace of God; lest any root of bitterness springing up trouble you, and thereby many be defiled

Hebrews 12:14–15

But if ye have bitter envying and strife in your hearts, glory not, and lie not against the truth

James 3:14

"Let him eschew evil, and do good; let him seek peace and pursue it"

1 Peter 3:11

WORK CITED

Amplified Bible, by B.B. Kirbridge Company, Inc. © 1908, 1917, 1929, 1964, 1982.

Dr. Ray Pritcharff, Forgiveness: healing the hurt we never deserve https://www.greekbiblestudy.org/gnt/main.

Personal experiences from members within my ministry

Quotes from Archbishop TuTu

King James Study Bible (previously published as the Liberty Annotated Study Bible and the Annotated Study Bible King James Version) © 1988. Liberty University.

Message Bible, 1995 by the Zondervan Corporation.

Myers, J. Stratight talk on stress. Warner Book Edition, © 1998 by Joyce Meyer.

Life in the word, Inc.

New Testament in Modern English ©1995 by the Zondervan Corporation.

Strong Concordance, by B.B. Kirbridge Company, Inc. © 1908, 1917, 1929, 1964, 1982.

www.dictionary.com

www.forgiveness.com/RdgRm.Quatationpage.com

www.tentmaker.org/Quotes/forgivenssquotes.htm